ADDING FRACTIONS

Third Edition

WORKBOOK

Ages 5-11, Grades K-5th grade and Years 1-6

Complete <u>blank spaces</u> with missing **fractions**, **equivalent** fractions, **decimal** fractions and **percentages**

Clear, concise and conveniently **illustrated** visual addition of fractions using basic *shapes and fractions association*. For visual learner children who are no fan of text-based fractions

Create your very own **fractions** to **complete**, **colour** & **shade** *(Blank shapes and equations templates provided)* ☺

Also available:

Colouring workbook: mybook.to/WB2-Sh   **Paperback**: mybook.to/B-2

Colour paperback: mybook.to/B2-C   **Colour ebook**: mybook.to/eB2-C

Workbook: mybook.to/WB2   Colour workbook: mybook.to/WB2-C

Free e-Book

MASTER MATHS FRACTIONS VISUALLY
FOR VISUAL LEARNER CHILDREN AND ADULTS WHO ARE STILL SCARED OF FRACTIONS

HATE FRACTIONS?

VISUAL MATHS FRACTIONS will change all that! *It is completely **Free** - nothing to lose to try it.*

This <u>visual</u> e-book will surprise you how easy it is to master maths fractions. **Download** it NOW!

Sign up for my **FREE** e-book and exclusive content @ FractionsVisually.com/

FractionsVisually.com

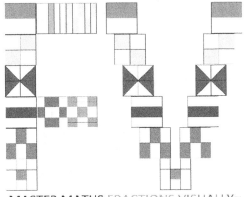

MASTER MATHS FRACTIONS VISUALLY™
For Folks Who Find Text-based
Fractions No Fun™
amazon.co.uk/FractionsVisually.com

Thank you for buying my book and helping me to keep on writing.
I hope you'll enjoy reading **ADDING** *FRACTIONS VISUALLY* WORKBOOK.
If so, please, kindly consider leaving a review on **Amazon.com** @
amazon.com/review/create-review?&asin=1729562493.
A single line, short sentence, few phrases or just rating will do.
No need to overthink of what to write, how much or how little.
If not, please, send me your feedback, comments and corrections to:
eng-s-jama@fractionsvisually.com.
Thanks.

Series 1: **UNDERSTANDING** FRACTIONS VISUALLY

Colouring workbook: mybook.to/WB1-Sh-v2   **Paperback**: mybook.to/B-1

Colour paperback: mybook.to/B1-C   **Colour ebook**: mybook.to/eB1-C

Workbook: mybook.to/WB-1   **Colour workbook**: mybook.to/WB1-C

Series 2: **ADDING** FRACTIONS VISUALLY

Colouring workbook: mybook.to/WB2-Sh   **Paperback**: mybook.to/B-2

Colour paperback: mybook.to/B2-C   **Colour ebook**: mybook.to/eB2-C

Workbook: mybook.to/WB2   **Colour workbook**: mybook.to/WB2-C

Series 3: **ADDING FRACTIONS** *STEP-**BY-**STEP*

Paperback: mybook.to/B-3   **Colour paperback**: mybook.to/B3-C

Workbook: mybook.to/WB3   **Colour workbook**: mybook.to/WB3-C

Series 4: **UNDERSTAND, ADD & SUBTRACT** FRACTIONS VISUALLY

Paperback: mybook.to/B-4   **Colour paperback**: mybook.to/B4-C

1

What is a **Fraction**?

A **fraction** is a **part** or **parts** of a whole.

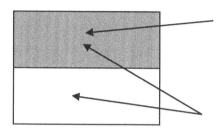

How many **parts** are **shaded** $\longrightarrow$

Fraction line $\longrightarrow$

Total parts (**shaded** + unshaded) $\longrightarrow$

$$\frac{1}{2}$$

- □ **Top** number (*numerator*) shows **how many parts** (out of a whole).

- □ Bottom number (*denominator*) shows *total* parts (to make 1 whole).

One part is shaded out of *two* parts.
That is a **half** or **one-half**.

$$\frac{1}{2}$$

Another part is unshaded out of two parts.
That is another half or one-half.

$$\frac{1}{2}$$

And $\quad \dfrac{1}{2}$ ☐ $+ \quad \dfrac{1}{2}$ ☐ $= \quad \dfrac{2}{2}$ ☐ $= \quad 1$ ☐

✓ A **proper fraction** is always *smaller* or *less than* a whole.

small   *medium*   *big*

A proper fraction can be: ☐ $\dfrac{1}{8}$, ☐ $\dfrac{1}{2}$ or ☐ $\dfrac{7}{8}$

But **not** as big as a whole like   or

Visual **Equivalent Fractions**

Equivalent means *equal in value*.

For example, if **2** children share **1** whole cake, they each get a **half**.

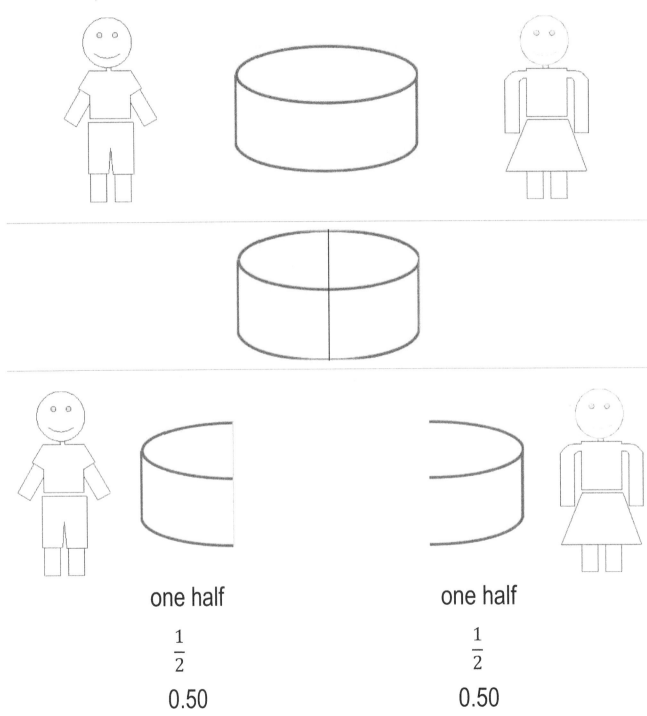

one half

$\dfrac{1}{2}$

0.50

one half

$\dfrac{1}{2}$

0.50

Also, if the same **two** children share *the same* whole cake, they can get **two quarters** each.
A **quarter** means one fourth of the whole. It is also **half** of a **half**.

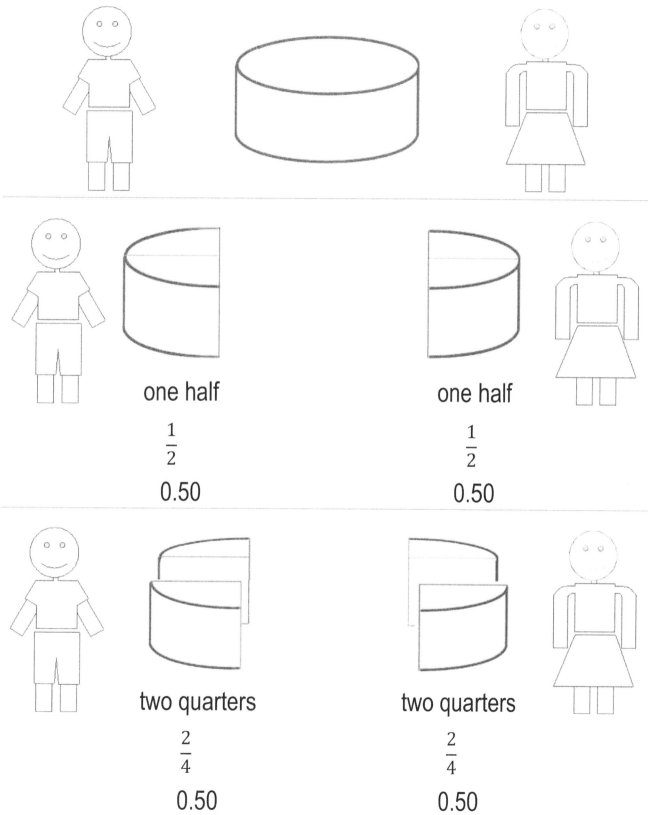

one half

$\dfrac{1}{2}$

0.50

one half

$\dfrac{1}{2}$

0.50

two quarters

$\dfrac{2}{4}$

0.50

two quarters

$\dfrac{2}{4}$

0.50

So, you can divide one whole cake into **two halves** (each child has a half) or into **four quarters** (every kid gets two quarters).

Therefore, one half is the same as **two quarters** — both equal to **0.50**.

$$\frac{1}{2} \ = \ \frac{2}{4} \ = \ 0.50 \ \rightarrow$$

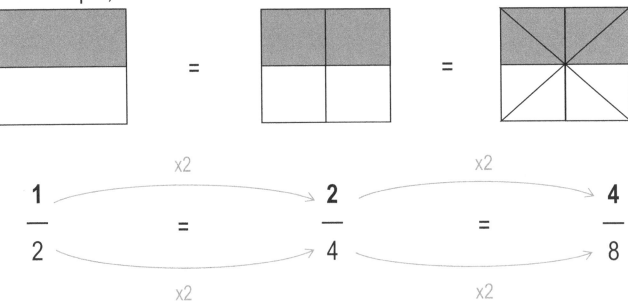

Equivalent fractions are fractions with the **same value** even though their **numerators** and **denominators** may be **different**.

For example,

That is, if you **multiply** (or *divide*) both the numerator and the denominator of a fraction by the same non-zero number, **the value** of that fraction **always stays the same**.

The fraction only changes into an *equivalent fraction* (which is the same total size).

This is because multiplying the top and the bottom of a fraction by the same non-zero number is the same as multiplying that fraction by 1.

This is the principle of **equivalent fractions**.

$$\frac{1}{2} \xrightarrow{\times 2} = \xrightarrow{\times 2} \frac{2}{4}$$

or ▢ $\times \dfrac{2}{2}$ (= ×1) = ▢

$$\frac{1}{2} \xrightarrow{\times 5} = \xrightarrow{\times 5} \frac{5}{10}$$

→ ▢ $\times \dfrac{5}{5}$ (= ×1) = ▢

$$\frac{1}{5} \xrightarrow{\times 2} = \xrightarrow{\times 2} \frac{2}{10}$$

or ▢ $\times \dfrac{2}{2}$ (= ×1) = ▢

$$\frac{1}{3} \xrightarrow{\times 2} = \xrightarrow{\times 2} \frac{2}{6} \xrightarrow{\times 3} = \xrightarrow{\times 3} \frac{6}{18}$$

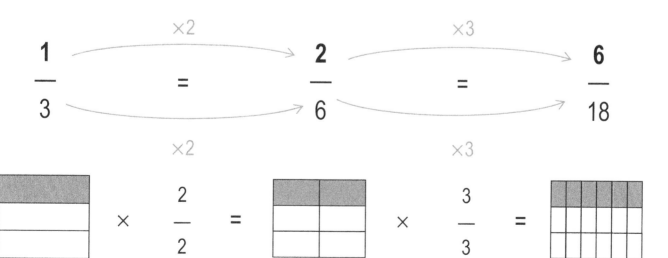

▢ $\times \dfrac{2}{2}$ = ▢ $\times \dfrac{3}{3}$ = ▢

And so on.

Fractions, Equivalent Fractions and Decimals

Equivalent fractions are fractions with the **same value** even though their **numerators** and **denominators** are **different**.

Halves, Quarters and Eighths

Complete blank spaces with missing equivalent fractions and decimals

Fractions to Equivalent Fractions						Decimals
$\dfrac{0}{2}$	=	$\dfrac{}{4}$	=	$\dfrac{}{8}$	=	0
		$\dfrac{1}{4}$	=	$\dfrac{}{8}$	=	---.------
$\dfrac{1}{2}$	=	$\dfrac{2}{}$	=	$\dfrac{}{8}$	=	0.50
		$\dfrac{3}{4}$	=	$\dfrac{}{8}$	=	---.------
$\dfrac{2}{}$	=	$\dfrac{}{4}$	=	$\dfrac{8}{}$	=	1.00

Fifths and Tenths

Complete blanks with missing equivalent fractions and decimal fractions

Fractions to Equivalent Fractions			Decimals
$\dfrac{0}{}$	=	$\dfrac{}{10}$	=	0
$\dfrac{}{5}$	=	$\dfrac{2}{10}$	=	---.------
$\dfrac{2}{5}$	=	$\dfrac{4}{}$	=	0.40
$\dfrac{}{5}$	=	$\dfrac{6}{10}$	=	---.------
$\dfrac{4}{5}$	=	$\dfrac{}{10}$	=	0.80
$\dfrac{}{5}$	=	$\dfrac{10}{10}$	=	---.------

10

Thirds, Sixths and Ninths

Complete blank spaces with missing equivalent fractions and decimals

Fractions to Equivalent Fractions			Decimals
$\dfrac{0}{3}$ = $\dfrac{\ }{6}$ = $\dfrac{\ }{9}$ =			0
$\dfrac{\ }{6}$ =			$0.16\overset{\cdot}{}$
$\dfrac{1}{3}$ = $\dfrac{\ }{6}$ = $\dfrac{3}{9}$ =			$\text{---.-----}\overset{\cdot}{}$
$\dfrac{3}{\ }$ =			0.50
$\dfrac{2}{3}$ = $\dfrac{4}{\ }$ = $\dfrac{\ }{9}$ =			$\text{---.-----}\overset{\cdot}{}$
$\dfrac{\ }{6}$ =			$0.83\overset{\cdot}{}$
$\dfrac{6}{6}$			
$\dfrac{\ }{3}$ = $\dfrac{\ }{6}$ = $\dfrac{\ }{9}$ =			1.00

$\overset{\cdot}{}$ means a **recurring** number — a number that keeps repeating for ever!
Example, $0.16\overset{\cdot}{} = 0.1666...$, $0.3\overset{\cdot}{} = 0.333...$, $0.6\overset{\cdot}{} = 0.666...$, $0.83\overset{\cdot}{} = 0.8333...$
etc.

Fractions, Decimals and Percentages

Halves, Quarters and Eighths

Complete blank spaces with missing fractions, decimals and percentages

Fractions to Equivalent Fractions			Decimals	Percentages

$$\frac{}{2} = \frac{0}{4} = \frac{}{8} = 0.00 = \text{-------}\%$$

$$\frac{1}{8} = \text{---.------} = 12.5\%$$

$$\frac{1}{4} = \frac{}{8} = \text{---.------} = \text{-------}\%$$

$$\frac{3}{} = 0.375 = \text{------.---}\%$$

12

Complete blank spaces with missing fractions, decimals and percentages

Fractions to Equivalent Fractions			Decimals	Percentages
$\dfrac{1}{2}$ = $\dfrac{}{4}$ = $\dfrac{4}{}$ =			---.------ =	50%
$\dfrac{}{8}$ =			0.625 =	------.---%
$\dfrac{3}{4}$ = $\dfrac{6}{}$ =			---.------ =	-------%
$\dfrac{7}{8}$ =			---.------ =	87.5%
$\dfrac{}{2}$ = $\dfrac{4}{}$ = $\dfrac{}{8}$ =			1.00 =	-------%

Fifths and Tenths

Complete blank spaces with missing fractions, decimals and percentages

Fractions to Equivalent Fractions				Decimals		Percentages
$\dfrac{}{5}$	=	$\dfrac{}{10}$	=	0.00	=	-------%
		$\dfrac{}{10}$	=	---.-------	=	10%
$\dfrac{1}{5}$	=	$\dfrac{2}{}$	=	0.20	=	-------%
		$\dfrac{}{10}$	=	---.-------	=	30%
$\dfrac{}{5}$	=	$\dfrac{4}{10}$	=	---.-------	=	------%
		$\dfrac{5}{}$	=	---.-------	=	50%

Fifths and Tenths

Complete blank spaces with missing fractions, decimals and percentages

Fractions to Equivalent Fractions			Decimals		Percentages
$\dfrac{3}{5}$	=	$\dfrac{6}{\rule{1.5em}{0.4pt}}$	=	---.------	=	------%
		$\dfrac{7}{10}$	=	---.------	=	70%
$\dfrac{\rule{1.5em}{0.4pt}}{5}$	=	$\dfrac{8}{\rule{1.5em}{0.4pt}}$	=	0.80	=	------%
		$\dfrac{9}{\rule{1.5em}{0.4pt}}$	=	---.------	=	90%
$\dfrac{\rule{1.5em}{0.4pt}}{5}$	=	$\dfrac{\rule{1.5em}{0.4pt}}{10}$	=	1.00	=	------%

Thirds, Sixths and Ninths

Complete blank spaces with missing fractions, decimals and percentages

Fractions to Equivalent Fractions			Decimals	Percentages
$\dfrac{0}{3}$ = $\dfrac{}{6}$ = $\dfrac{}{9}$ =			0.00 =	-----%
$\dfrac{}{9}$ =			---.------˙ =	11.1˙%
$\dfrac{2}{}$ =			0.222˙ =	------.---˙%
$\dfrac{1}{3}$ = $\dfrac{2}{}$ = $\dfrac{}{9}$ =			---.------˙ =	33.3˙%
$\dfrac{4}{}$ =			0.444˙ =	------.---˙%

˙ shows a **recurring** number, which keeps repeating for ever!

Example, 11.1˙ = 11.111..., 22.2˙ = 22.222..., 33.3˙ = 33.333...,

44.4˙ = 44.444... etc.

Thirds, Sixths and Ninths

Complete blank spaces with missing fractions, decimals and percentages

Fractions to Equivalent Fractions			Decimals	Percentages
$\dfrac{5}{\underline{}}$			$= 0.555^{\cdot}$	$= \underline{}.\underline{}^{\cdot}\%$
$\dfrac{2}{\underline{}} = \dfrac{\underline{}}{6} = \dfrac{6}{9}$			$= \underline{}.\underline{}^{\cdot}$	$= 66.6^{\cdot}\%$
$\dfrac{\underline{}}{9}$			$= 0.777^{\cdot}$	$= \underline{}.\underline{}^{\cdot}\%$
$\dfrac{\underline{}}{9}$			$= \underline{}.\underline{}^{\cdot}$	$= 88.8^{\cdot}\%$
$\dfrac{3}{\underline{}} = \dfrac{6}{6} = \dfrac{\underline{}}{9}$			$= 1.00$	$= 100\%$

$^{\cdot}$ indicates a **recurring** number that never ends, but keeps repeating forever.
Examples: $55.5^{\cdot} = 55.555...$, $66.6^{\cdot} = 66.666...$, $77.7^{\cdot} = 77.777...$,
$88.8^{\cdot} = 88.888...$ and so on.

Adding **Halves**

Complete the following visual fraction additions.

Fill in blank spaces with missing **fractions**, fraction **names** and **decimal** fractions

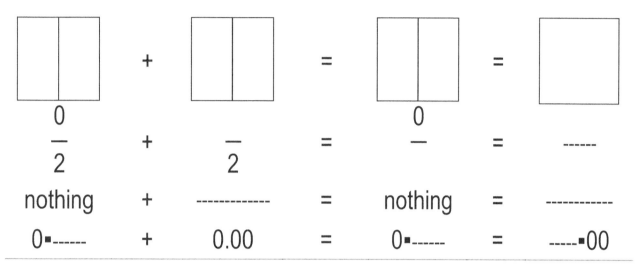

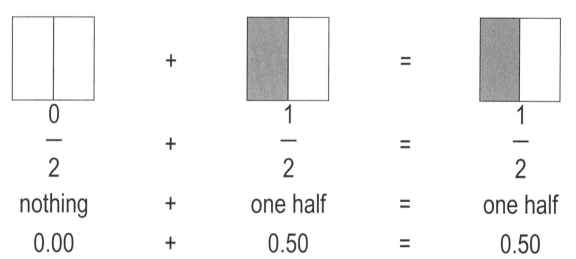

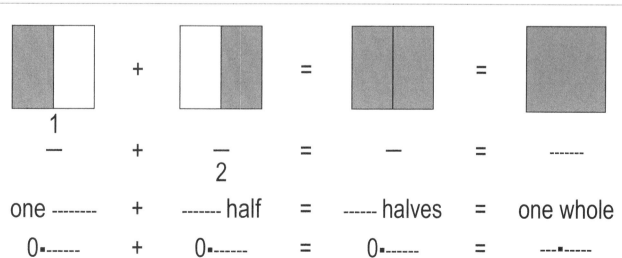

Adding **Quarters**

Complete the following visual fraction additions.
Fill in blanks with missing **fractions**, fraction **names** and **decimal** fractions

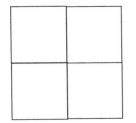 + 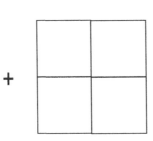 = 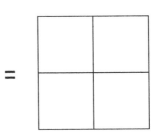 =

$$\frac{0}{4} \quad + \quad \frac{0}{4} \quad = \quad \frac{0}{4} \quad = \quad 0$$

nothing   +   nothing   =   nothing   =   nothing

0.00   +   0.00   =   0.00   =   0

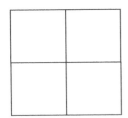 + 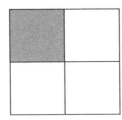 =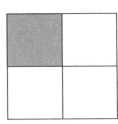

$$\frac{}{4} \quad + \quad \frac{1}{} \quad = \quad \frac{}{}$$

_____   +   one
                           _____   =   _____

---•____   +   ---•___   =   ---•___

19

Complete the following visual fraction additions.

Fill in blanks with missing **fractions**, fraction **names** and **decimal** fractions

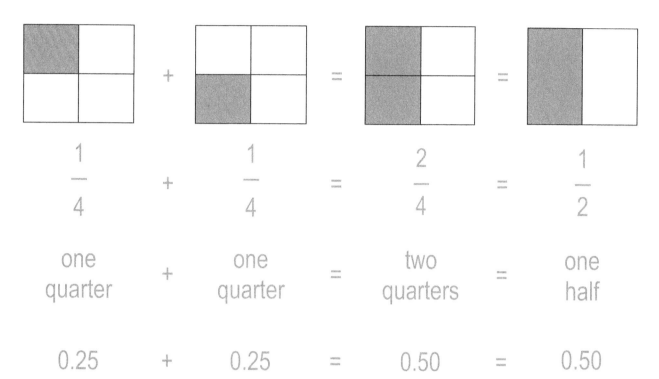

$$\frac{1}{4} \quad + \quad \frac{1}{4} \quad = \quad \frac{2}{4} \quad = \quad \frac{1}{2}$$

| one quarter | + | one quarter | = | two quarters | = | one half |

0.25   +   0.25   =   0.50   =   0.50

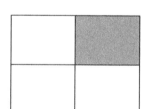   +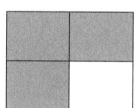

___   +   ___   =   ___   =   ___

___   +   ___   =   ___   =   ___

___   +   ___   =   ___   =   ___

Complete the following visual fraction additions.
Fill in blanks with missing **fractions**, fraction **names** and **decimal** fractions

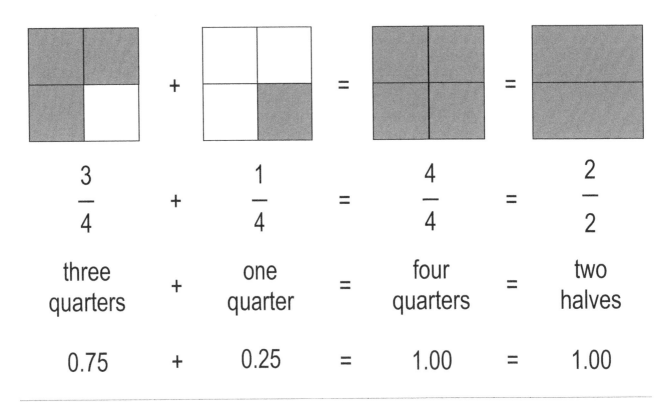

$\dfrac{3}{4}$	+	$\dfrac{1}{4}$	=	$\dfrac{4}{4}$	=	$\dfrac{2}{2}$
three quarters	+	one quarter	=	four quarters	=	two halves
0.75	+	0.25	=	1.00	=	1.00

―	+	―	=	―	=	------
---------------- + -----------------	+	-------------- ------------------	=	-------------- ------------------	=	one --------------
---•-------	+	---•-------	=	---•------	=	---•-----

Adding **Eighths**

Complete the following visual fraction additions.
Fill in blanks with missing **fractions**, fraction **names** and **decimal** fractions

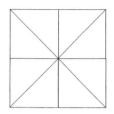   +   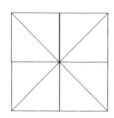   =   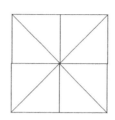   =

$$\frac{0}{8}$$ + $$\frac{0}{8}$$ = $$\frac{0}{8}$$ =   0

nothing   +   nothing   =   nothing   =   nothing

0.00   +   0.00   =   0.00   =   0

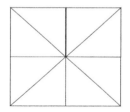   +   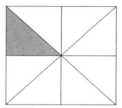   =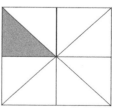

—   +   —   =   —

_____   +   one   =   _____
                        _____   _____

---∎-------   +   ---∎-------   =   ---∎-------

22

Complete the following visual fraction additions.
Fill in blanks with missing **fractions**, fraction **names** and **decimal** fractions

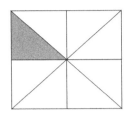 + 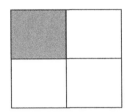 = =

$$\frac{1}{8} \quad + \quad \frac{1}{8} \quad = \quad \frac{2}{8} \quad = \quad \frac{1}{4}$$

one
eighth   +   one
eighth   =   two
eighths   =   one
quarter

0.125   +   0.125   =   0.250   =   0.25

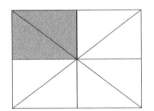 + 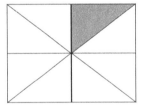 =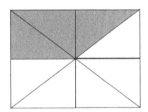

—   +   —   =   —

------------   +   ------------   =   ------------
------------   ------------   ------------

---■------   +   ---■------   =   ---■------

Complete the following visual fraction additions.
Fill in blanks with missing **fractions**, fraction **names** and **decimal** fractions

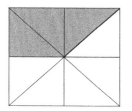 + 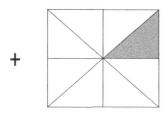 = 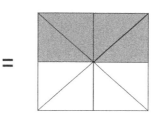 =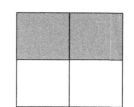

$$\frac{3}{8} \quad + \quad \frac{1}{8} \quad = \quad \frac{4}{8} \quad = \quad \frac{2}{4}$$

| three eighths | + | one eighth | = | four eighths | = | two quarters |

0.375   +   0.125   =   0.50   =   0.50

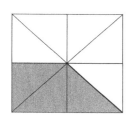 + 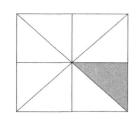 = 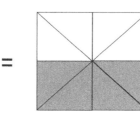 =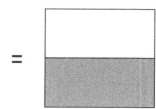

$$\frac{\quad}{\quad} \quad + \quad \frac{\quad}{\quad} \quad = \quad \frac{\quad}{\quad} \quad = \quad \frac{\quad}{\quad}$$

-------------- + -------------- = -------------- = --------------
--------------   --------------   --------------   --------------

---■--------- + ---■--------- = ---■--------- = ---■-------

Complete the following visual fraction additions.
Fill in blanks with missing **fractions**, fraction **names** and **decimal** fractions

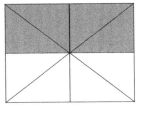 + 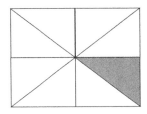 =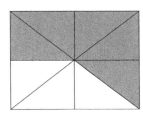

$$\frac{4}{8} \quad + \quad \frac{1}{8} \quad = \quad \frac{5}{8}$$

| four eighths | + | one eighth | = | five eighths |

$$0.50 \quad + \quad 0.125 \quad = \quad 0.625$$

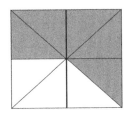 + 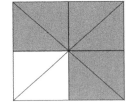 = + =

$$- \quad + \quad - \quad = \quad - \quad = \quad \frac{}{4}$$

$$\text{------} \quad + \quad \text{------} \quad = \quad \text{------} \quad = \quad \text{------}$$

25

Complete the following visual fraction additions.
Fill in blanks with missing **fractions**, fraction **names** and **decimal** fractions

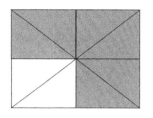 + 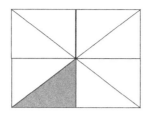 =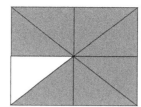

$$\frac{6}{8} \quad + \quad \frac{1}{8} \quad = \quad \frac{7}{8}$$

six
eighths

+

one
eighth

=

seven
eighths

0.75 + 0.125 = 0.875

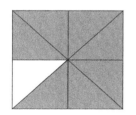 + 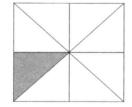 = 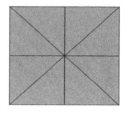 =

—   +   —   =   —   =   --------

--------------- + --------------- = --------------- = -----------
--------------- --------------- --------------- whole

---■--------- + ---■--------- = ---■--------- = ---■---------

Halves + Quarters

Complete the following visual fraction additions.
Fill in blank spaces with missing fractions and decimal fractions, as applicable

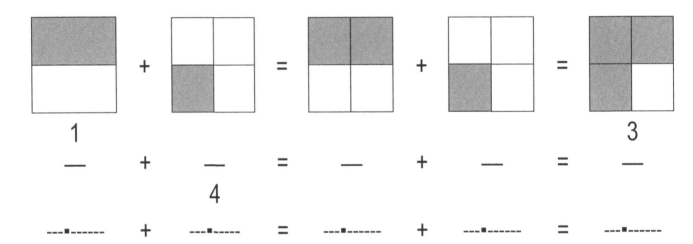

$$\frac{0}{2} + \frac{0}{4} = \frac{0}{4} + \frac{0}{4} = \frac{0}{4} = 0$$

$$0.00 \;+\; 0.00 \;=\; 0.00 \;+\; 0.00 \;=\; 0.00 \;=\; 0$$

$$\frac{1}{} + \frac{}{4} = \frac{}{} + \frac{}{} = \frac{3}{}$$

$$\text{----}\blacksquare\text{----} \;+\; \text{----}\blacksquare\text{----} \;=\; \text{----}\blacksquare\text{----} \;+\; \text{----}\blacksquare\text{----} \;=\; \text{----}\blacksquare\text{----}$$

$$\frac{}{} + \frac{}{} = \frac{}{} + \frac{}{} = \frac{}{} = \text{------}$$

$$\text{----}\blacksquare\text{----} \;+\; \text{----}\blacksquare\text{----} \;=\; \text{----}\blacksquare\text{----} \;+\; \text{----}\blacksquare\text{----} \;=\; \text{----}\blacksquare\text{----} \;=\; \text{----}\blacksquare\text{----}$$

Quiz 1

Match fractions with their **sums** (see **example** given).

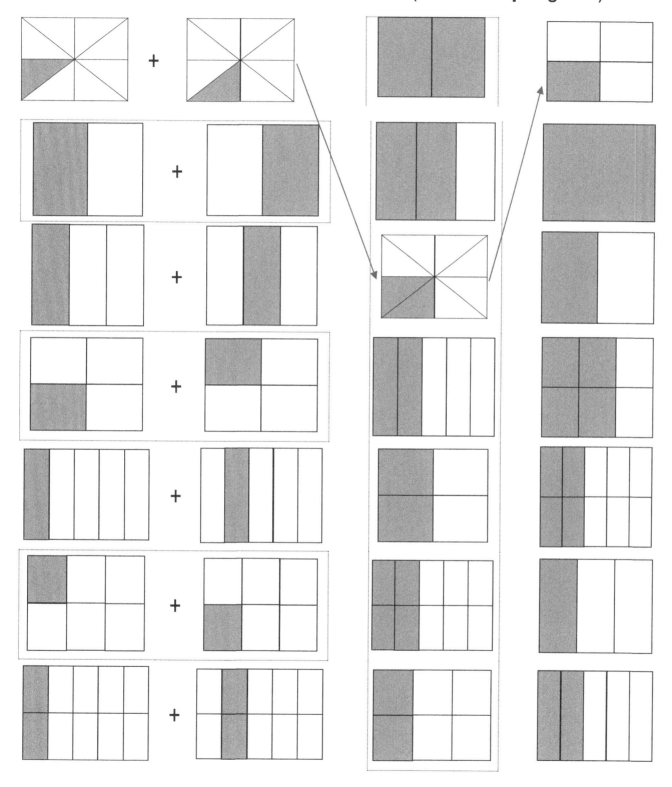

28

Halves + Eighths

Complete the following visual fraction additions.
Fill in blanks with missing fractions and decimal fractions, as applicable

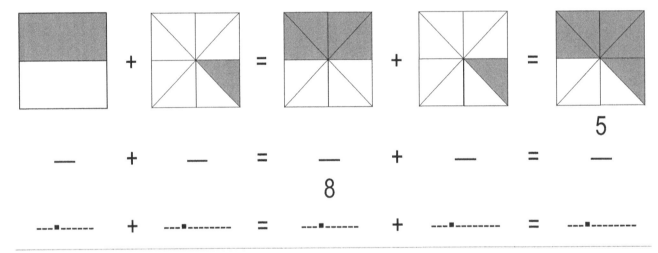

$$\frac{0}{2} + \frac{0}{8} = \frac{0}{8} + \frac{0}{8} = \frac{0}{8} = 0$$

$$0.00 + 0.00 = 0.00 + 0.00 = 0.00 = 0$$

$$— + — = \frac{—}{8} + — = \frac{5}{—}$$

$$\text{---}\blacksquare\text{-------} + \text{---}\blacksquare\text{---------} = \text{---}\blacksquare\text{-------} + \text{---}\blacksquare\text{---------} = \text{---}\blacksquare\text{---------}$$

$$— + — = — + — = — = —$$

$$\text{---}\blacksquare\text{-------} + \text{---}\blacksquare\text{-------} = \text{---}\blacksquare\text{-------} + \text{---}\blacksquare\text{-------} = \text{---}\blacksquare\text{-------} = \text{---}\blacksquare\text{-------}$$

29

Complete the following visual fraction additions.
Fill in blank spaces with missing fractions and decimal fractions, as applicable

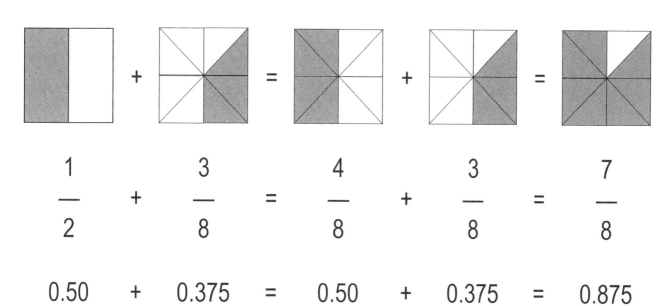

$$\frac{1}{2} \;+\; \frac{3}{8} \;=\; \frac{4}{8} \;+\; \frac{3}{8} \;=\; \frac{7}{8}$$

0.50 + 0.375 = 0.50 + 0.375 = 0.875

— + — = — + — = — = ------

---■------ + ---■------ = ---■------ + ---■------ = ---■------ = ---■------

30

Quarters + Eighths

Complete the following visual fraction additions.
Fill in blanks with missing fractions and decimal fractions, as applicable

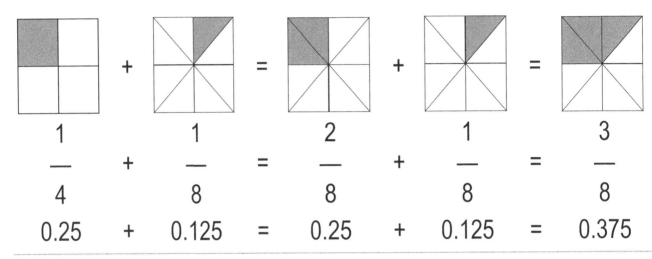

$$\frac{1}{4} \;+\; \frac{1}{8} \;=\; \frac{2}{8} \;+\; \frac{1}{8} \;=\; \frac{3}{8}$$

$$0.25 \;+\; 0.125 \;=\; 0.25 \;+\; 0.125 \;=\; 0.375$$

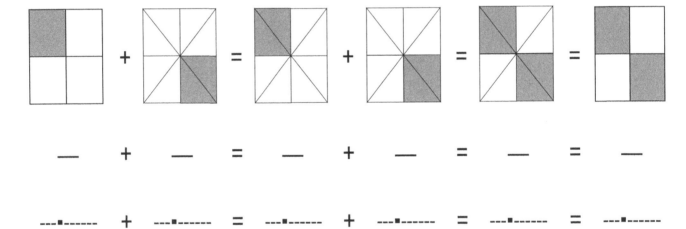

$$\underline{} \;+\; \underline{} \;=\; \underline{} \;+\; \underline{} \;=\; \underline{} \;=\; \underline{}$$

$$\text{----} \;+\; \text{----} \;=\; \text{----} \;+\; \text{----} \;=\; \text{----} \;=\; \text{----}$$

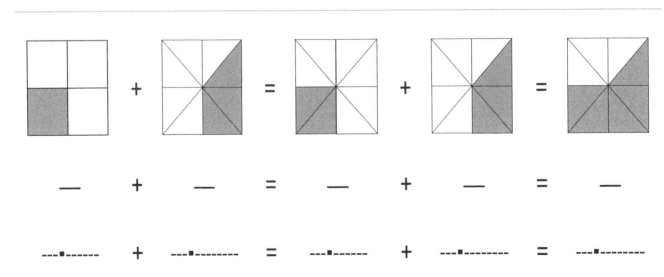

$$\underline{} \;+\; \underline{} \;=\; \underline{} \;+\; \underline{} \;=\; \underline{}$$

$$\text{----} \;+\; \text{----} \;=\; \text{----} \;+\; \text{----} \;=\; \text{----}$$

Complete the following visual fraction additions.
Fill in blank spaces with missing fractions and decimal fractions, as applicable

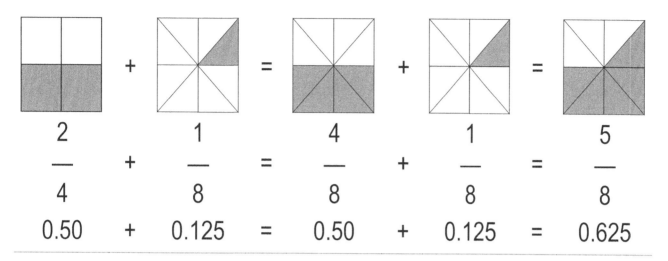

$$\frac{2}{4} + \frac{1}{8} = \frac{4}{8} + \frac{1}{8} = \frac{5}{8}$$

$$0.50 + 0.125 = 0.50 + 0.125 = 0.625$$

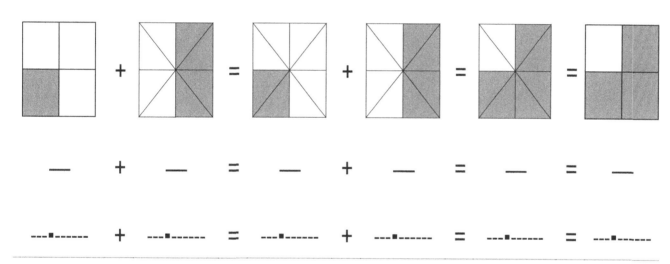

$$\frac{\quad}{\quad} + \frac{\quad}{\quad} = \frac{\quad}{\quad} + \frac{\quad}{\quad} = \frac{\quad}{\quad} = \frac{\quad}{\quad}$$

$$\text{----} + \text{----} = \text{----} + \text{----} = \text{----} = \text{----}$$

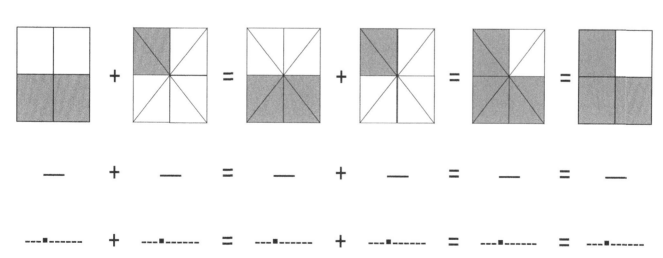

$$\frac{\quad}{\quad} + \frac{\quad}{\quad} = \frac{\quad}{\quad} + \frac{\quad}{\quad} = \frac{\quad}{\quad} = \frac{\quad}{\quad}$$

$$\text{----} + \text{----} = \text{----} + \text{----} = \text{----} = \text{----}$$

Complete the following visual fraction additions.

Fill in blanks with missing fractions and decimal fractions, as applicable

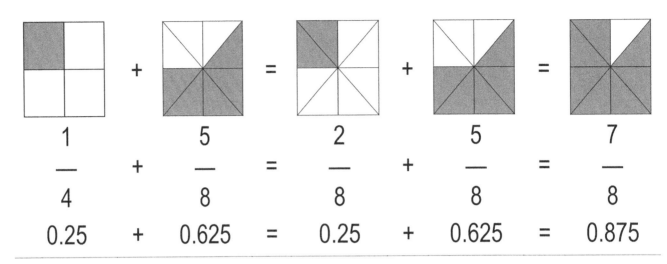

$$\frac{1}{4} + \frac{5}{8} = \frac{2}{8} + \frac{5}{8} = \frac{7}{8}$$

$$0.25 + 0.625 = 0.25 + 0.625 = 0.875$$

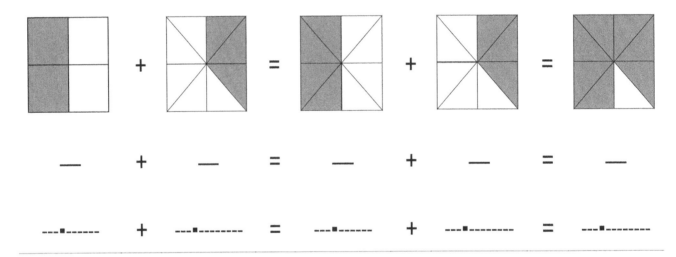

$$\frac{}{} + \frac{}{} = \frac{}{} + \frac{}{} = \frac{}{}$$

----■------- + ----■--------- = ----■------- + ----■--------- = ----■---------

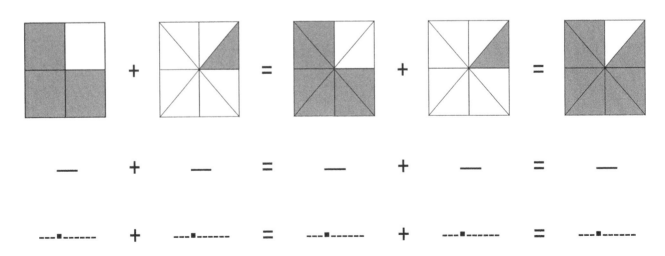

$$\frac{}{} + \frac{}{} = \frac{}{} + \frac{}{} = \frac{}{}$$

----■------- + ----■------- = ----■------- + ----■------- = ----■-------

Complete the following visual fraction additions.

Fill in blank spaces with missing fractions and decimal fractions, as applicable

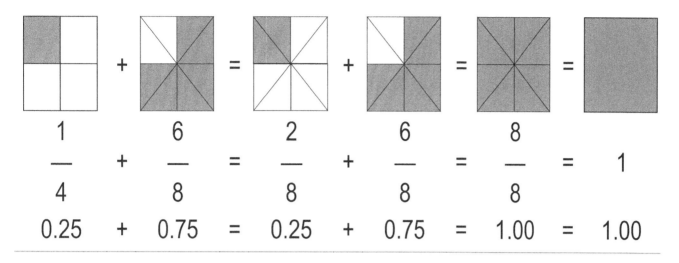

	1		6		2		6		8		
	$\dfrac{1}{4}$	+	$\dfrac{6}{8}$	=	$\dfrac{2}{8}$	+	$\dfrac{6}{8}$	=	$\dfrac{8}{8}$	=	1
	0.25	+	0.75	=	0.25	+	0.75	=	1.00	=	1.00

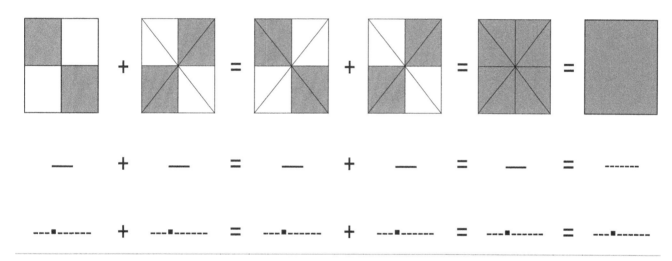

$$\underline{} \quad + \quad \underline{} \quad = \quad \underline{} \quad + \quad \underline{} \quad = \quad \underline{} \quad = \quad \text{------}$$

$$\text{----■------} \quad + \quad \text{---■------} \quad = \quad \text{---■------} \quad + \quad \text{----■------} \quad = \quad \text{---■------} \quad = \quad \text{---■------}$$

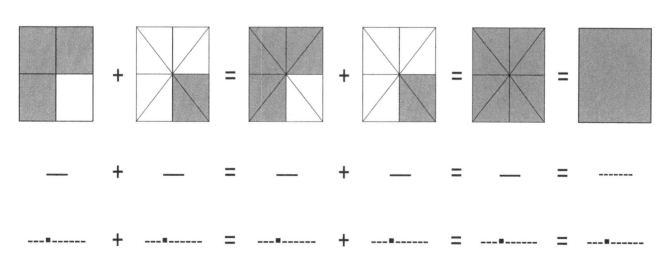

$$\underline{} \quad + \quad \underline{} \quad = \quad \underline{} \quad + \quad \underline{} \quad = \quad \underline{} \quad = \quad \text{------}$$

$$\text{---■------} \quad + \quad \text{---■------} \quad = \quad \text{---■------} \quad + \quad \text{---■------} \quad = \quad \text{---■------} \quad = \quad \text{---■------}$$

Halves + Quarters + Eighths

Complete the following visual fraction additions.
Fill in blanks with missing fractions and decimal fractions, as applicable

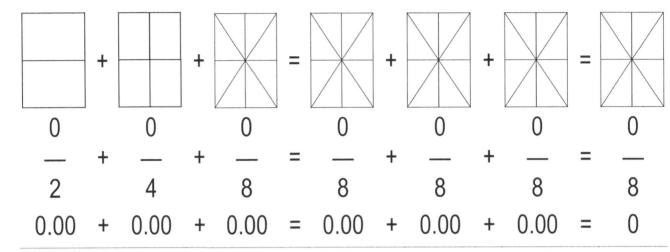

$$\frac{0}{2} + \frac{0}{4} + \frac{0}{8} = \frac{0}{8} + \frac{0}{8} + \frac{0}{8} = \frac{0}{8}$$

$$0.00 + 0.00 + 0.00 = 0.00 + 0.00 + 0.00 = 0$$

1   7

$$\frac{}{} + \frac{}{} + \frac{}{8} = \frac{}{} + \frac{}{} + \frac{}{} = \frac{}{}$$

---■----- + --■----- + ---■----- = --■----- + --■------ + ---■----- = ---■------

$$\frac{}{} + \frac{}{} + \frac{}{} = \frac{}{} + \frac{}{} + \frac{}{} = \frac{}{} = \text{-------}$$

--■--- + --■--- + --■--- = --■--- + --■--- + --■--- = --■--- = --■---

35

Adding **Fifths**

Complete the following visual fraction additions.
Fill in blanks with missing **fractions**, fraction **names** and **decimal** fractions

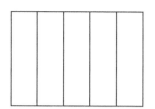 + 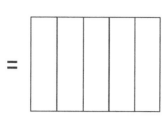 =   =

$$\frac{0}{5} + \frac{0}{5} = \frac{0}{5} = 0$$

nothing   +   nothing   =   nothing   =   nothing

0.00   +   0.00   =   0.00   =   0

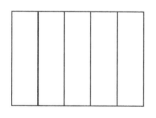   +   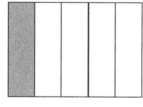   =

$- \quad + \quad \dfrac{1}{-} \quad = \quad -$

---------------   + $\dfrac{\text{----------}}{\text{--------------}}$ = $\dfrac{\text{----------}}{\text{--------------}}$

---■------   +   0.20   =   ---■------

Complete the following visual fraction additions.
Fill in blanks with missing **fractions**, fraction **names** and **decimal** fractions

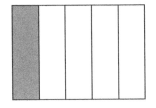 + 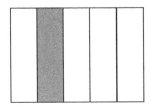 =

$$\frac{1}{5} \quad + \quad \frac{1}{5} \quad = \quad \frac{2}{5}$$

one
fifth
+
one
fifth
=
two
fifths

0.20 + 0.20 = 0.40

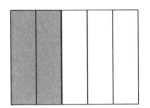 + 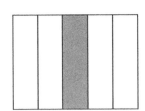 =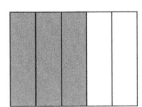

— + — = —

------------ + ------------ = ------------
------------ ------------ ------------

---∎------- + ---∎------- = ---∎-------

37

Complete the following visual fraction additions.
Fill in blanks with missing **fractions**, fraction **names** and **decimal** fractions

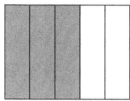   +   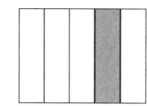   =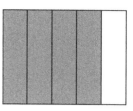

$$\frac{3}{5}$$ + $$\frac{1}{5}$$ = $$\frac{4}{5}$$

three
fifths   +   one
fifth   =   four
fifths

0.60   +   0.20   =   0.80

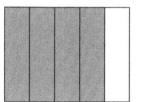   +   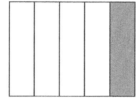   =   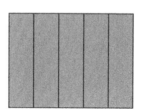   =

—   +   —   =   —   =   -------

---------   +   ----------   =   ----------   =   one

---------   +   ----------   =   ----------   =   ----------

---■------   +   ---■------   =   ---■------   =   ---■------

Adding **Tenths**

Complete the following visual fraction additions.
Fill in blanks with missing **fractions**, fraction **names** and **decimal** fractions

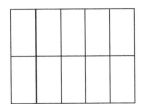 + 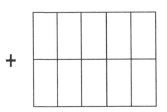 = 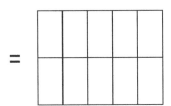 =

$$\frac{0}{10} \quad + \quad \frac{0}{10} \quad = \quad \frac{0}{10} \quad = \quad 0$$

nothing   +   nothing   =   nothing   =   nothing

0.00   +   0.00   =   0.00   =   0

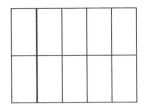 + 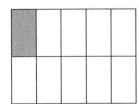 =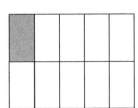

$$\frac{}{10} \quad + \quad \frac{1}{} \quad = \quad \frac{}{}$$

\-\-\-\-\-\-\-\-\-\-\-\-\-\-   + $\dfrac{\text{----------}}{\text{---------------}}$ = $\dfrac{\text{----------}}{\text{tenth}}$

\-\-\-■\-\-\-\-\-   +   \-\-\-■\-\-\-\-   =   \-\-\-■\-\-\-\-

39

Complete the following visual fraction additions.
Fill in blanks with missing **fractions**, fraction **names** and **decimal** fractions

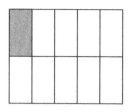 + 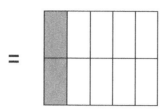 =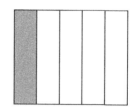

$\dfrac{1}{10}$ + $\dfrac{1}{10}$ = $\dfrac{2}{10}$ = $\dfrac{1}{5}$

one
tenth + one
tenth = two
tenths = one
fifth

0.10 + 0.10 = 0.20 = 0.20

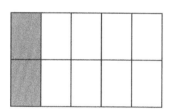 + 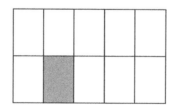 =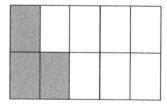

— + — = —

----------- + ---------- = ----------
--------------- --------------- ---------------

---■------- + ---■------- = ---■-------

40

Complete the following visual fraction additions.
Fill in blanks with missing **fractions**, fraction **names** and **decimal** fractions

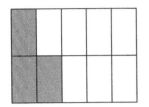 + 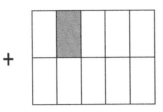 = 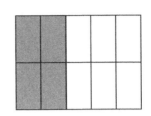 =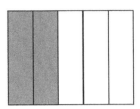

$$\frac{3}{10} \quad + \quad \frac{1}{10} \quad = \quad \frac{4}{10} \quad = \quad \frac{2}{5}$$

three tenths	+	one tenth	=	four tenths	=	two fifths

0.30   +   0.10   =   0.40   =   0.40

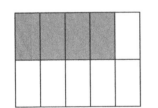 + 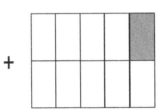 = 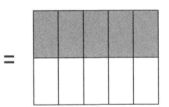 =

$$\text{—} \quad + \quad \text{—} \quad = \quad \text{—} \quad = \quad \frac{}{2}$$

---------- + ---------- = ---------- = ----------

---■------- + ---■------- = ---■------- = ---■-------

Complete the following visual fraction additions.
Fill in blanks with missing **fractions**, fraction **names** and **decimal** fractions

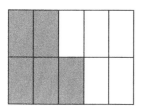 + 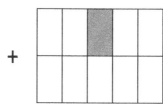 = 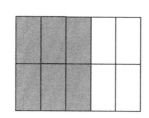 =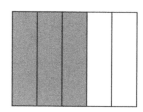

$$\frac{5}{10} \quad + \quad \frac{1}{10} \quad = \quad \frac{6}{10} \quad = \quad \frac{3}{5}$$

| five tenths | + | one tenth | = | six tenths | = | three fifths |

0.50   +   0.10   =   0.60   =   0.60

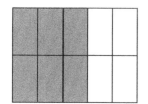 + 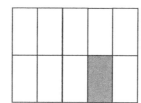 =

$$\frac{}{} \quad + \quad \frac{}{} \quad = \quad \frac{}{}$$

---------   ---------   ---------
+   =
---------------   ---------------   ---------------

---∎------   +   ---∎------   =   ---∎------

Complete the following visual fraction additions.
Fill in blanks with missing **fractions**, fraction **names** and **decimal** fractions

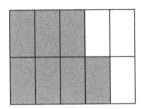 + 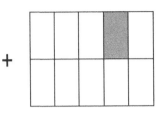 = 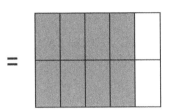 =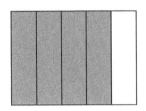

$$\frac{7}{10}$$ + $$\frac{1}{10}$$ = $$\frac{8}{10}$$ = $$\frac{4}{5}$$

seven
tenths
+
one
tenth
=
eight
tenths
=
four
fifths

0.70 + 0.10 = 0.80 = 0.80

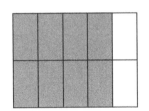 + 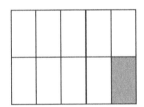 =

— + — = —

---------- + ---------- = ----------
---------- ---------- ----------

---∎------ + ---∎------ = ---∎------

43

Complete the following visual fraction additions.
Fill in blanks with missing **fractions**, fraction **names** and **decimal** fractions

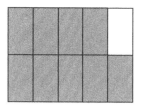 + 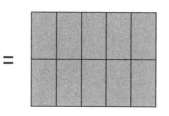 =  =

$$\frac{9}{10} \quad + \quad \frac{1}{10} \quad = \quad \frac{10}{10} \quad = \quad 1$$

| nine tenths | + | one tenth | = | ten tenths | = | one, whole |

0.90   +   0.10   =   1.00   =   1.00

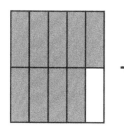 + 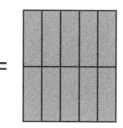 = 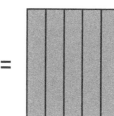 = 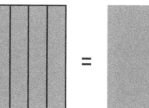 =

— + — = — = — = -------

--------- + --------- = --------- = --------- = one
---------   ---------   ---------   ---------   ---------

---■----- + ---■----- = ---■----- = ---■----- = ---■-----

Fifths + Tenths

Complete the following visual fraction additions.

Fill in blanks with missing fractions and decimal fractions, as applicable

$$\frac{0}{5} + \frac{0}{10} = \frac{0}{10} + \frac{0}{10} = \frac{0}{10} = 0$$

$$0.00 + 0.00 = 0.00 + 0.00 = 0.00 = 0$$

$$\frac{}{} + \frac{}{} = \frac{}{} + \frac{}{} = \frac{}{}$$

$$\underline{\quad} + \underline{\quad} = \underline{\quad} + \underline{\quad} = \underline{\quad}$$

$$\frac{}{} + \frac{}{} = \frac{}{} + \frac{}{} = \frac{}{} = \frac{}{}$$

$$\underline{\quad} + \underline{\quad} = \underline{\quad} + \underline{\quad} = \underline{\quad} = \underline{\quad}$$

45

Complete the following visual fraction additions.
Fill in blank spaces with missing fractions and decimal fractions, as applicable

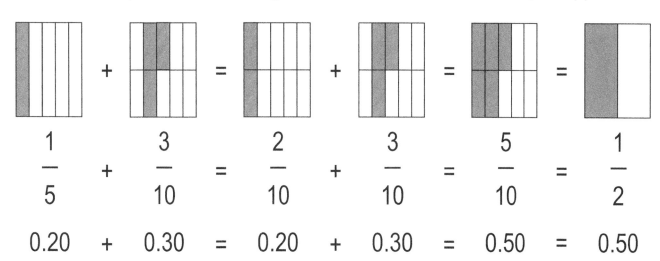

$$\frac{1}{5} + \frac{3}{10} = \frac{2}{10} + \frac{3}{10} = \frac{5}{10} = \frac{1}{2}$$

0.20 + 0.30 = 0.20 + 0.30 = 0.50 = 0.50

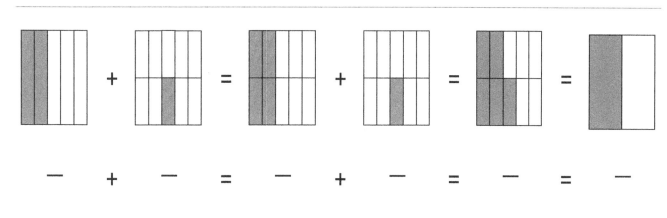

— + — = — + — = — = —

---■------- + ---■------- = ---■------- + ---■------- = ---■------- = ---■-------

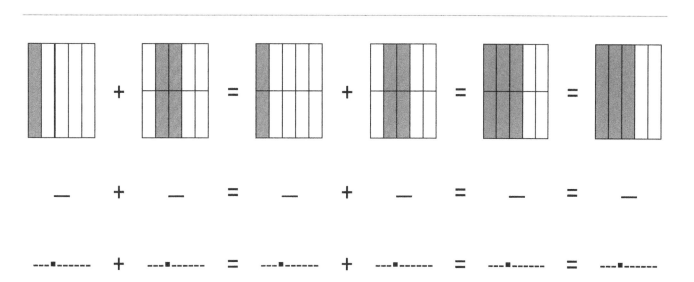

— + — = — + — = — = —

---■------- + ---■------- = ---■------- + ---■------- = ---■------- = ---■-------

Complete the following visual fraction additions.
Fill in blanks with missing fractions and decimal fractions, as applicable

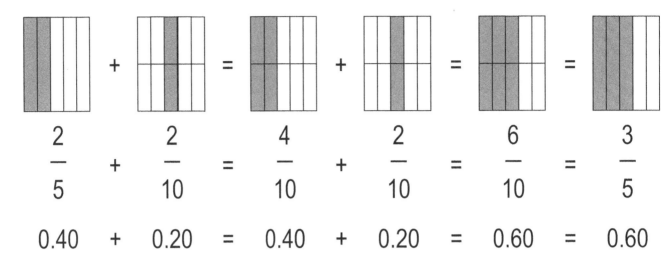

$$\frac{2}{5} + \frac{2}{10} = \frac{4}{10} + \frac{2}{10} = \frac{6}{10} = \frac{3}{5}$$

$$0.40 + 0.20 = 0.40 + 0.20 = 0.60 = 0.60$$

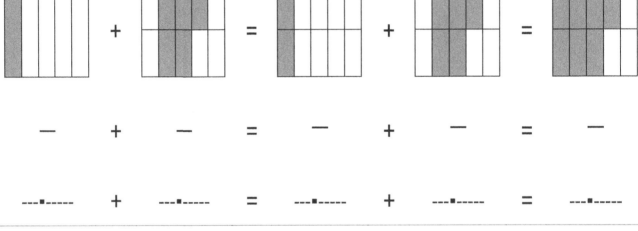

$$\frac{}{} + \frac{}{} = \frac{}{} + \frac{}{} = \frac{}{}$$

____·____ + ____·____ = ____·____ + ____·____ = ____·____

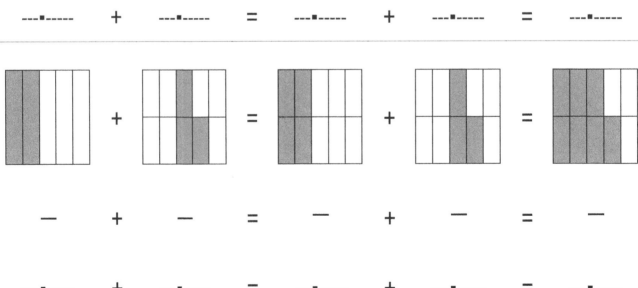

$$\frac{}{} + \frac{}{} = \frac{}{} + \frac{}{} = \frac{}{}$$

____·____ + ____·____ = ____·____ + ____·____ = ____·____

Complete the following visual fraction additions.
Fill in blank spaces with missing fractions and decimal fractions, as applicable

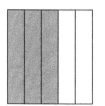 + 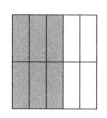 = 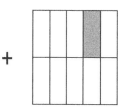 + 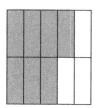 =

$$\frac{3}{5} + \frac{1}{10} = \frac{6}{10} + \frac{1}{10} = \frac{7}{10}$$

0.60 + 0.10 = 0.60 + 0.10 = 0.70

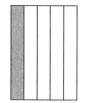 + 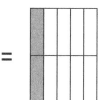 = 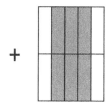 + 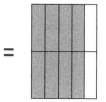 =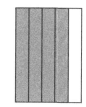

— + — = — + — = —

---■------ + ---■------ = ---■------ + ---■------ = ---■------ = ---■------

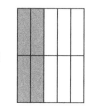 + 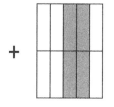 = 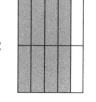 + =

— + — = — + — = —

---■------ + ---■------ = ---■------ + ---■------ = ---■------ = ---■------

Complete the following visual fraction additions.
Fill in blanks with missing fractions and decimal fractions, as applicable

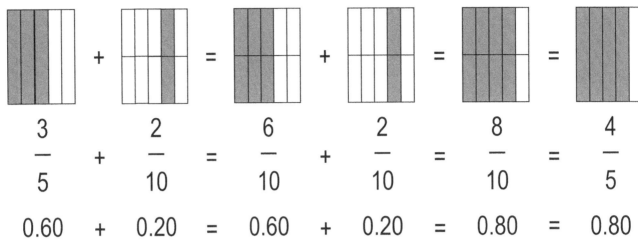

$$\frac{3}{5} + \frac{2}{10} = \frac{6}{10} + \frac{2}{10} = \frac{8}{10} = \frac{4}{5}$$

0.60 + 0.20 = 0.60 + 0.20 = 0.80 = 0.80

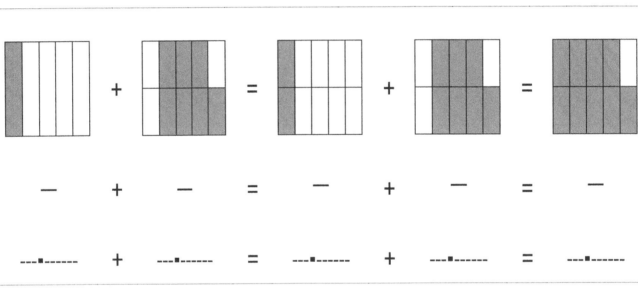

$$\frac{}{} + \frac{}{} = \frac{}{} + \frac{}{} = \frac{}{}$$

----■------- + ----■------- = ----■------- + ----■------- = ----■-------

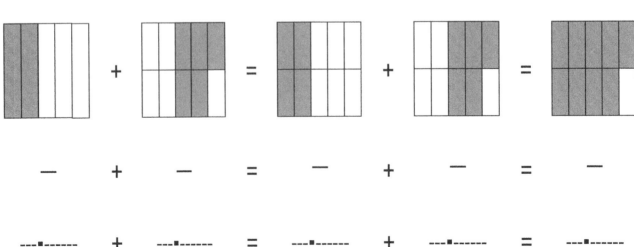

$$\frac{}{} + \frac{}{} = \frac{}{} + \frac{}{} = \frac{}{}$$

----■------- + ----■------- = ----■------- + ----■------- = ----■-------

Complete the following visual fraction additions.
Fill in blank spaces with missing fractions and decimal fractions, as applicable

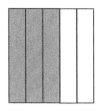 + 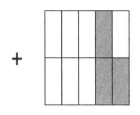 = 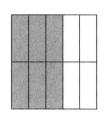 + 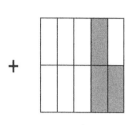 =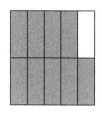

$$\frac{3}{5} + \frac{3}{10} = \frac{6}{10} + \frac{3}{10} = \frac{9}{10}$$

0.60 + 0.30 = 0.60 + 0.30 = 0.90

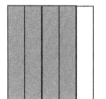 +  = 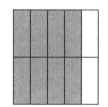 + 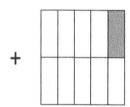 =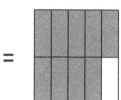

$$- \quad + \quad - \quad = \quad - \quad + \quad - \quad = \quad -$$

 + = + =

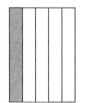 + 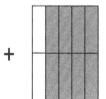 = 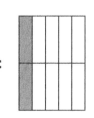 + 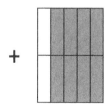 = 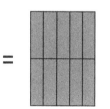 =

$$- \quad + \quad - \quad = \quad - \quad + \quad - \quad = \quad - \quad = \quad \text{-------}$$

 + = + ----■----- = ----■----- =

50

Complete the following visual fraction additions.
Fill in blanks with missing fractions and decimal fractions, as applicable

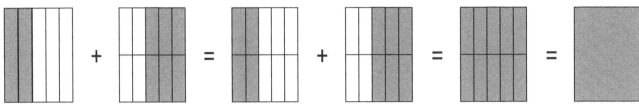

$$\frac{2}{5} + \frac{6}{10} = \frac{4}{10} + \frac{6}{10} = \frac{10}{10} = 1$$

$$0.40 + 0.60 = 0.40 + 0.60 = 1.00 = 1.00$$

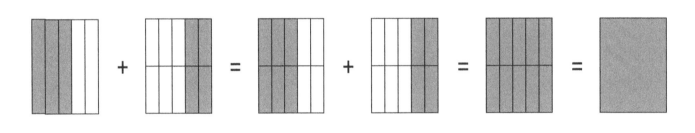

$$— + — = — + — = — = \text{-------}$$

$$\text{---}\blacksquare\text{-------} + \text{---}\blacksquare\text{-------} = \text{---}\blacksquare\text{-------} + \text{---}\blacksquare\text{-------} = \text{---}\blacksquare\text{-------} = \text{---}\blacksquare\text{-------}$$

$$— + — = — + — = — = 1$$

$$\text{---}\blacksquare\text{-------} + \text{---}\blacksquare\text{-------} = \text{---}\blacksquare\text{-------} + \text{---}\blacksquare\text{-------} = \text{---}\blacksquare\text{-------} = \text{---}\blacksquare\text{-------}$$

Adding **Thirds**

Complete the following visual fraction additions.
Fill in blanks with missing **fractions**, fraction **names** and **decimal** fractions

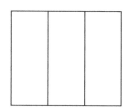 + = =

$$\frac{0}{3} \quad + \quad \frac{0}{3} \quad = \quad \frac{0}{3} \quad = \quad 0$$

nothing + nothing = nothing = nothing

0.00 + 0.00 = 0.00 = 0

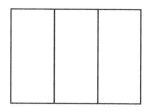 + 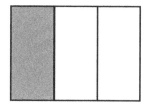 =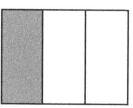

— + — = —

------------ + ------- = -------
              ------------   ------------

---■------· + ---■-----· = ---■-----·

Complete the following visual fraction additions.
Fill in blanks with missing **fractions**, fraction **names** and **decimal** fractions

$$\frac{1}{3} \quad + \quad \frac{1}{3} \quad = \quad \frac{2}{3}$$

one third $\quad + \quad$ one third $\quad = \quad$ two thirds

$0.3^{.} \quad + \quad 0.3^{.} \quad = \quad 0.6^{.}$

$$— \quad + \quad — \quad = \quad — \quad = \quad \text{-----}$$

$$\frac{\text{-------}}{\text{-----------}} \quad + \quad \frac{\text{-------}}{\text{-----------}} \quad = \quad \frac{\text{-------}}{\text{-----------}} \quad = \quad \frac{\text{one}}{\text{-----------}}$$

$$\text{---■-----}^{.} \quad + \quad \text{---■-----}^{.} \quad = \quad \text{---■-----}^{.} \quad = \quad \text{---■-----}^{.}$$

Adding **Sixths**

Complete the following visual fraction additions.
Fill in blanks with missing **fractions**, fraction **names** and **decimal** fractions

 + 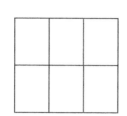 = 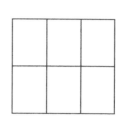 =

$$\frac{0}{6} \quad + \quad \frac{0}{6} \quad = \quad \frac{0}{6} \quad = \quad 0$$

nothing   +   nothing   =   nothing   =   nothing

0.00   +   0.00   =   0.00   =   0

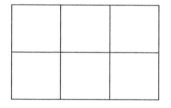 + 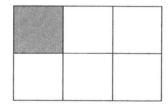 =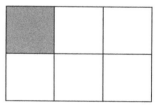

$$\frac{\quad}{6} \quad + \quad \frac{1}{\quad} \quad = \quad \frac{\quad}{\quad}$$

------------   + $\dfrac{--------}{------------}$ = $\dfrac{------}{------------}$

---■------·   +   ---■-----·   =   ---■------·

Complete the following visual fraction additions.
Fill in blanks with missing **fractions**, fraction **names** and **decimal** fractions

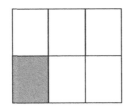

$$\frac{1}{6} + \frac{1}{6} = \frac{2}{6} = \frac{1}{3}$$

| one sixth | + | one sixth | = | two sixths | = | one third |

$$0.16\dot{} \quad + \quad 0.16\dot{} \quad = \quad 0.3\dot{} \quad = \quad 0.3\dot{}$$

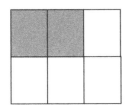 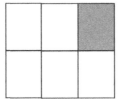 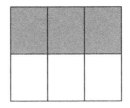 

$$\frac{}{} + \frac{}{} = \frac{}{} = \frac{}{}$$

----------   ----------   ----------   ----------
----------   +   ----------   =   ----------   =   ----------

___■___˙   +   ___■___˙   =   ___■___˙   =   ___■___

Complete the following visual fraction additions.
Fill in blanks with missing **fractions**, fraction **names** and **decimal** fractions

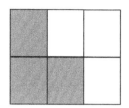

$$\frac{3}{6} \quad + \quad \frac{1}{6} \quad = \quad \frac{4}{6} \quad = \quad \frac{2}{3}$$

| three sixths | + | one sixth | = | four sixths | = | two thirds |

0.50   +   0.16˙   =   0.6˙   =   0.6˙

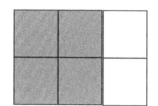   +   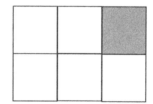   =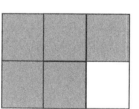

—   +   —   =   —

-------------   +   -------------   =   -------------
-------------   -------------   -------------

---■-------˙   +   ---■-------˙   =   ---■-------˙

Complete the following visual fraction additions.
Fill in blanks with missing **fractions**, fraction **names** and **decimal** fractions

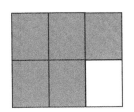   +   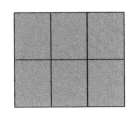   =   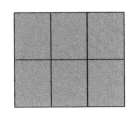   =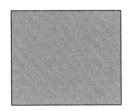

$$\frac{5}{6} \quad + \quad \frac{1}{6} \quad = \quad \frac{6}{6} \quad = \quad 1$$

five
sixths   +   one
sixth   =   six
sixths   =   one
whole

0.83˙   +   0.16˙   =   1.00   =   1.00

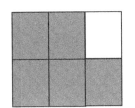   +   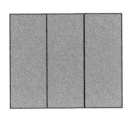   =      =

$$\text{---} \quad + \quad \text{---} \quad = \quad \frac{3}{\text{---}} \quad = \quad \text{-------}$$

$$\frac{\text{-----------}}{\text{-----------}} \quad + \quad \frac{\text{-----------}}{\text{-----------}} \quad = \quad \frac{\text{-----------}}{\text{-----------}} \quad = \quad \frac{\text{-----------}}{\text{-----------}}$$

___.___˙   +   ___.___˙   =   ___.___   =   ___.___

Adding **Ninths**

Complete the following visual fraction additions.
Fill in blanks with missing **fractions**, fraction **names** and **decimal** fractions

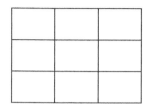 + 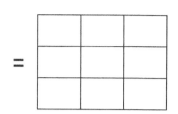 = 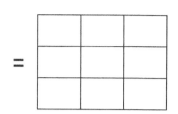 =

$$\frac{0}{9} \quad + \quad \frac{0}{9} \quad = \quad \frac{0}{9} \quad = \quad 0$$

nothing   +   nothing   =   nothing   =   nothing

0.00   +   0.00   =   0.00   =   0

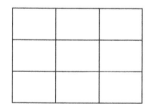 + 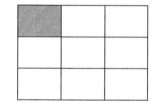 =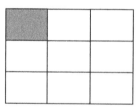

—   +   —   =   —

-------------   +   -------------   =   -------------

---■------- `    +    ---■------- `   =   ---■------- `

Complete the following visual fraction additions.
Fill in blanks with missing **fractions**, fraction **names** and **decimal** fractions

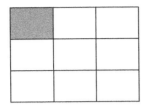 + 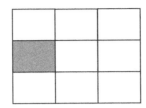 =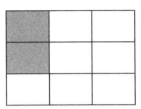

$$\frac{1}{9}$$ + $$\frac{1}{9}$$ = $$\frac{2}{9}$$

one
ninth + one
ninth = two
ninths

0.1˙ + 0.1˙ = 0.2˙

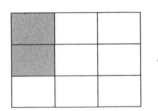 + 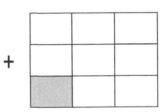 = 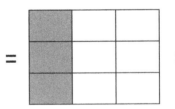 =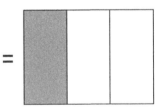

— + — = — = —

‒‒‒‒‒‒‒ + ‒‒‒‒‒‒ = ‒‒‒‒‒‒ = ‒‒‒‒‒‒
‒‒‒‒‒‒‒‒   ‒‒‒‒‒‒   ‒‒‒‒‒‒   ‒‒‒‒‒‒

‒‒∎‒‒‒˙ + ‒‒∎‒‒‒˙ = ‒‒∎‒‒‒˙ = ‒‒∎‒‒‒˙

Complete the following visual fraction additions.
Fill in blanks with missing **fractions**, fraction **names** and **decimal** fractions

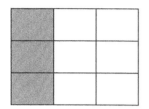 + 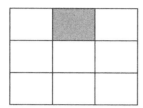 =

$$\frac{3}{9} \qquad + \qquad \frac{1}{9} \qquad = \qquad \frac{4}{9}$$

three
ninths
+
one
ninth
=
four
ninths

0.3˙ + 0.1˙ = 0.4˙

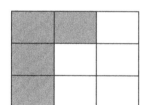 + 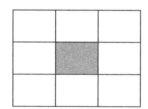 =

$$— \qquad + \qquad — \qquad = \qquad —$$

+

=

---∎-------˙ + ---∎-------˙ = ---∎-------˙

60

Complete the following visual fraction additions.
Fill in blanks with missing **fractions**, fraction **names** and **decimal** fractions

 + 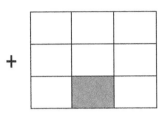 = 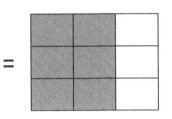 =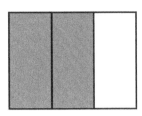

$$\frac{5}{9} \quad + \quad \frac{1}{9} \quad = \quad \frac{6}{9} \quad = \quad \frac{2}{3}$$

| five ninths | + | one ninth | = | six ninths | = | two thirds |

$$0.\dot{5} \quad + \quad 0.\dot{1} \quad = \quad 0.\dot{6} \quad = \quad 0.\dot{6}$$

 + 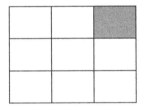 =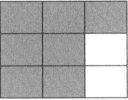

$$- \quad + \quad - \quad = \quad -$$

$$\frac{\text{------------}}{\text{------------}} \quad + \quad \frac{\text{------------}}{\text{------------}} \quad = \quad \frac{\text{------------}}{\text{------------}}$$

$$\text{---}\blacksquare\text{------}^{\cdot} \quad + \quad \text{---}\blacksquare\text{------}^{\cdot} \quad = \quad \text{---}\blacksquare\text{------}^{\cdot}$$

Complete the following visual fraction additions.
Fill in blanks with missing **fractions**, fraction **names** and **decimal** fractions

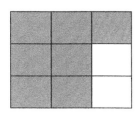 + 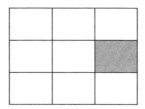 =

$$\frac{7}{9}$$ + $$\frac{1}{9}$$ = $$\frac{8}{9}$$

seven
ninths
+
one
ninth
=
eight
ninths

0.7˙ + 0.1˙ = 0.8˙

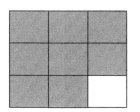 +  = 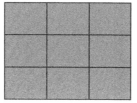 =

— + — = — = -------

$$\frac{\rule{1cm}{0.4pt}}{\rule{1cm}{0.4pt}}$$ + $$\frac{\rule{1cm}{0.4pt}}{\rule{1cm}{0.4pt}}$$ = $$\frac{\rule{1cm}{0.4pt}}{\rule{1cm}{0.4pt}}$$ = $$\frac{\rule{1cm}{0.4pt}}{\text{whole}}$$

---•------˙ + ---•------˙ = ---•------ = ---•------

Thirds + Sixths

Complete the following visual fraction additions.
Fill in blanks with missing fractions and decimal fractions, as applicable

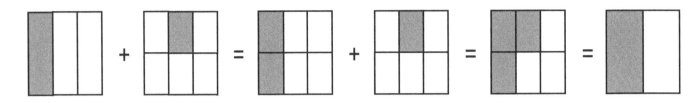

$$\frac{1}{3} + \frac{1}{6} = \frac{2}{6} + \frac{1}{6} = \frac{3}{6} = \frac{1}{2}$$

$$0.3^{\cdot} + 0.16^{\cdot} = 0.3^{\cdot} + 0.16^{\cdot} = 0.50 = 0.50$$

— + — = — + — = — = —

..·.......· + ..·.......· = ..·.......· + ..·.......· = ..·.......· = ..·.......·

Complete the following visual fraction additions.

Fill in blank spaces with missing fractions and decimal fractions, as applicable

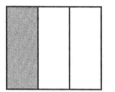

$$\frac{1}{3} \quad + \quad \frac{3}{6} \quad = \quad \frac{2}{6} \quad + \quad \frac{3}{6} \quad = \quad \frac{5}{6}$$

$$0.3\dot{} \quad + \quad 0.50 \quad = \quad 0.3\dot{} \quad + \quad 0.50 \quad = \quad 0.83\dot{}$$

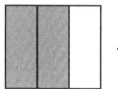 + 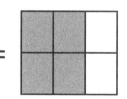 = 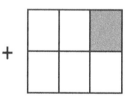 +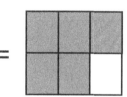

$$\underline{\quad} \quad + \quad \underline{\quad} \quad = \quad \underline{\quad} \quad + \quad \underline{\quad} \quad = \quad \underline{\quad}$$

Complete the following visual fraction additions.

Fill in blanks with missing fractions and decimal fractions, as applicable

$$\frac{1}{3} + \frac{4}{6} = \frac{2}{6} + \frac{4}{6} = \frac{6}{6} = 1$$

$$0.3^{\cdot} + 0.6^{\cdot} = 0.3^{\cdot} + 0.6^{\cdot} = 1.00 = 1.00$$

$$\underline{} + \underline{} = \underline{} + \underline{} = \underline{} = \underline{}$$

$$\underline{}^{\cdot} + \underline{}^{\cdot} = \underline{}^{\cdot} + \underline{}^{\cdot} = \underline{} = \underline{}$$

Thirds + Ninths

Complete the following visual fraction additions.
Fill in blank spaces with missing fractions and decimal fractions, as applicable

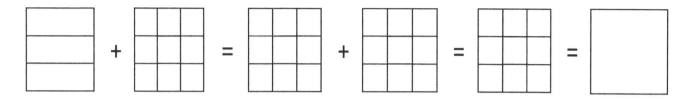

$$\frac{0}{3} \;+\; \frac{0}{9} \;=\; \frac{0}{9} \;+\; \frac{0}{9} \;=\; \frac{0}{9} \;=\; 0$$

$$0.00 \;+\; 0.00 \;=\; 0.00 \;+\; 0.00 \;=\; 0.00 \;=\; 0$$

$$\text{—} \;+\; \text{—} \;=\; \text{—} \;+\; \text{—} \;=\; \text{—}$$

$$\text{\_\_.\_\_\_\_.} \;+\; \text{\_\_.\_\_\_\_.} \;=\; \text{\_\_.\_\_\_\_.} \;+\; \text{\_\_.\_\_\_\_.} \;=\; \text{\_\_.\_\_\_\_.}$$

Complete the following visual fraction additions.
Fill in blanks with missing fractions and decimal fractions, as applicable

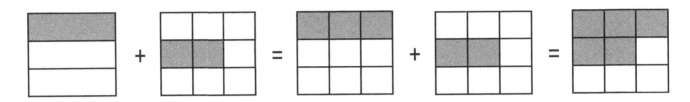

$$\frac{1}{3} \quad + \quad \frac{2}{9} \quad = \quad \frac{3}{9} \quad + \quad \frac{2}{9} \quad = \quad \frac{5}{9}$$

$$0.\dot{3} \quad + \quad 0.\dot{2} \quad = \quad 0.\dot{3} \quad + \quad 0.\dot{2} \quad = \quad 0.\dot{5}$$

$$— \quad + \quad — \quad = \quad — \quad + \quad — \quad = \quad — \quad = \quad —$$

$$\text{--.------} \quad + \quad \text{--.------} \quad = \quad \text{--.------} \quad + \quad \text{--.------} \quad = \quad \text{--.------} \quad = \quad \text{--.------}$$

Complete the following visual fraction additions.
Fill in blank spaces with missing fractions and decimal fractions, as applicable

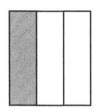 + 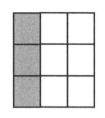 = ☐ + ☐ =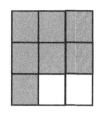

$$\frac{1}{3} + \frac{4}{9} = \frac{3}{9} + \frac{4}{9} = \frac{7}{9}$$

$$0.3\dot{} + 0.4\dot{} = 0.3\dot{} + 0.4\dot{} = 0.7\dot{}$$

☐ + ☐ = ☐ + ☐ = ☐

$$\frac{}{} + \frac{}{} = \frac{}{} + \frac{}{} = \frac{}{}$$

$$\_\_\cdot\_\_\_\dot{} \; + \; \_\_\cdot\_\_\_\dot{} \; = \; \_\_\cdot\_\_\_\dot{} \; + \; \_\_\cdot\_\_\_\dot{} \; = \; \_\_\cdot\_\_\_\dot{}$$

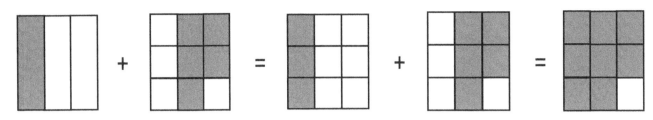

Complete the following visual fraction additions.
Fill in blanks with missing fractions and decimal fractions, as applicable

$$\frac{1}{3} \quad + \quad \frac{5}{9} \quad = \quad \frac{3}{9} \quad + \quad \frac{5}{9} \quad = \quad \frac{8}{9}$$

$$0.\dot{3} \quad + \quad 0.\dot{5} \quad = \quad 0.\dot{3} \quad + \quad 0.\dot{5} \quad = \quad 0.\dot{8}$$

— + — = — + — = —

--∎------˙ + --∎------˙ = --∎------˙ + --∎------˙ = --∎------˙

Complete the following visual fraction additions.
Fill in blank spaces with missing fractions and decimal fractions, as applicable

$$\frac{1}{3} + \frac{6}{9} = \frac{3}{9} + \frac{6}{9} = \frac{9}{9} = 1$$

$$0.3\dot{} + 0.6\dot{} = 0.3\dot{} + 0.6\dot{} = 1.00 = 1.00$$

$$\frac{\quad}{\quad} + \frac{\quad}{\quad} = \frac{\quad}{\quad} + \frac{\quad}{\quad} = \frac{\quad}{\quad} = \text{-------}$$

$$\text{--}\blacksquare\text{----}\dot{} + \text{--}\blacksquare\text{----}\dot{} = \text{--}\blacksquare\text{----}\dot{} + \text{--}\blacksquare\text{----}\dot{} = \text{--}\blacksquare\text{----} = \text{--}\blacksquare\text{----}$$

Sixths + Ninths

Complete the following visual fraction additions.
Fill in blanks with missing fractions and decimal fractions, as applicable

$$\frac{0}{6} + \frac{0}{9} = \frac{0}{18} + \frac{0}{18} = \frac{0}{18} = 0$$

$$0.00 + 0.00 = 0.00 + 0.00 = 0.00 = 0$$

$$\frac{1}{\quad} + \frac{\quad}{\quad} = \frac{\quad}{18} + \frac{\quad}{\quad} = \frac{5}{\quad}$$

$$\text{.\!...\!.....} + 0.1\dot{} = \text{.\!...\!.....} + 0.1\dot{} = \text{.\!...\!.....}$$

71

Complete the following visual fraction additions.
Fill in blank spaces with missing fractions and decimal fractions, as applicable

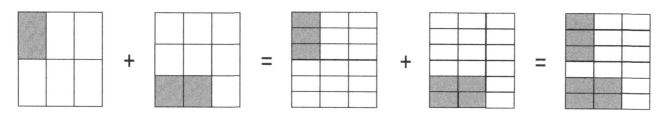

$$\frac{1}{6} \quad + \quad \frac{2}{9} \quad = \quad \frac{3}{18} \quad + \quad \frac{4}{18} \quad = \quad \frac{7}{18}$$

$$0.1\dot{6} \quad + \quad 0.\dot{2} \quad = \quad 0.1\dot{6} \quad + \quad 0.\dot{2} \quad = \quad 0.3\dot{8}$$

$$\frac{\quad}{\quad} \quad + \quad \frac{\quad}{\quad} \quad = \quad \frac{\quad}{\quad} \quad + \quad \frac{\quad}{\quad} \quad = \quad \frac{\quad}{\quad} \quad = \quad \frac{\quad}{\quad}$$

72

Complete the following visual fraction additions.
Fill in blanks with missing fractions and decimal fractions, as applicable

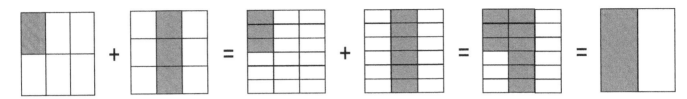

$$\frac{1}{6} + \frac{3}{9} = \frac{3}{18} + \frac{6}{18} = \frac{9}{18} = \frac{1}{2}$$

$$0.16^{\cdot} + 0.3^{\cdot} = 0.16^{\cdot} + 0.3^{\cdot} = 0.50 = 0.50$$

$$\frac{}{} + \frac{}{} = \frac{}{} + \frac{}{} = \frac{}{} = \frac{}{}$$

$$\underline{\quad}.\underline{\quad}^{\cdot} + \underline{\quad}.\underline{\quad}^{\cdot} = \underline{\quad}.\underline{\quad}^{\cdot} + \underline{\quad}.\underline{\quad}^{\cdot} = \underline{\quad}.\underline{\quad}^{\cdot} = \underline{\quad}.\underline{\quad}^{\cdot}$$

Complete the following visual fraction additions.
Fill in blank spaces with missing fractions and decimal fractions, as applicable

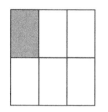 + 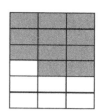 = 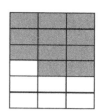 + 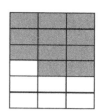 =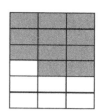

$$\frac{1}{6} + \frac{4}{9} = \frac{3}{18} + \frac{8}{18} = \frac{11}{18}$$

0.16˙ + 0.4˙ = 0.16˙ + 0.4˙ = 0.61˙

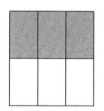 + 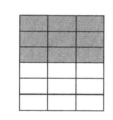 = 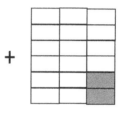 + 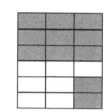 =

— + — = — + — = —

--■----˙ + --■----˙ = --■----˙ + --■----˙ = --■----˙

74

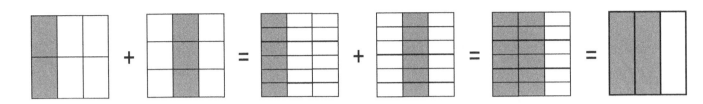

$$\frac{2}{6} \quad + \quad \frac{3}{9} \quad = \quad \frac{6}{18} \quad + \quad \frac{6}{18} \quad = \quad \frac{12}{18} \quad = \quad \frac{2}{3}$$

$$0.\overset{.}{3} \quad + \quad 0.\overset{.}{3} \quad = \quad 0.\overset{.}{3} \quad + \quad 0.\overset{.}{3} \quad = \quad 0.\overset{.}{6} \quad = \quad 0.\overset{.}{6}$$

$$\underline{} \quad + \quad \underline{} \quad = \quad \underline{} \quad + \quad \underline{} \quad = \quad \underline{}$$

$$\underline{}. \quad + \quad \underline{}. \quad = \quad \underline{}. \quad + \quad \underline{}. \quad = \quad \underline{}.$$

Complete the following visual fraction additions.
Fill in blank spaces with missing fractions and decimal fractions, as applicable

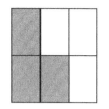 + 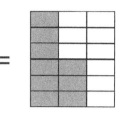 = 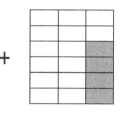 + 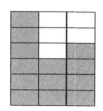 =

$$\frac{3}{6} + \frac{2}{9} = \frac{9}{18} + \frac{4}{18} = \frac{13}{18}$$

0.50 + 0.2˙ = 0.50 + 0.2˙ = 0.72˙

 + 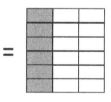 = 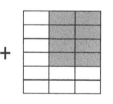 + 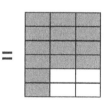 =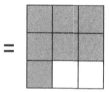

$$\frac{\quad}{\quad} + \frac{\quad}{\quad} = \frac{\quad}{\quad} + \frac{\quad}{\quad} = \frac{\quad}{\quad} = \frac{\quad}{\quad}$$

--■-----˙ + --■-----˙ = --■-----˙ + --■-----˙ = --■-----˙ = --■-----˙

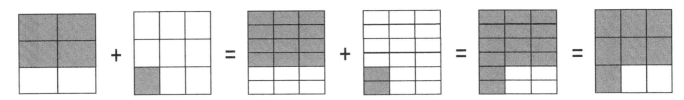

$$\frac{4}{6} + \frac{1}{9} = \frac{12}{18} + \frac{2}{18} = \frac{14}{18} = \frac{7}{9}$$

$$0.6\dot{} + 0.1\dot{} = 0.6\dot{} + 0.1\dot{} = 0.7\dot{} = 0.7\dot{}$$

$$\frac{}{} + \frac{}{} = \frac{}{} + \frac{}{} = \frac{}{} = \frac{}{}$$

$$\_\_\bullet\_\_\_\dot{} + \_\_\bullet\_\_\_\dot{} = \_\_\bullet\_\_\_\dot{} + \_\_\bullet\_\_\_\dot{} = \_\_\bullet\_\_\_\dot{} = \_\_\bullet\_\_\_\dot{}$$

Complete the following visual fraction additions.
Fill in blank spaces with missing fractions and decimal fractions, as applicable

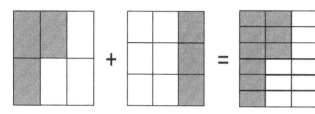

$$\frac{3}{6} + \frac{3}{9} = \frac{9}{18} + \frac{6}{18} = \frac{15}{18} = \frac{5}{6}$$

$$0.50 + 0.3\dot{} = 0.50 + 0.3\dot{} = 0.83\dot{} = 0.83\dot{}$$

$$\frac{}{} + \frac{}{} = \frac{}{} + \frac{}{} = \frac{}{} = \frac{}{}$$

$$\_\_\_\_\dot{} + \_\_\_\_\dot{} = \_\_\_\_\dot{} + \_\_\_\_\dot{} = \_\_\_\_\dot{} = \_\_\_\_\dot{}$$

Complete the following visual fraction additions.
Fill in blanks with missing fractions and decimal fractions, as applicable

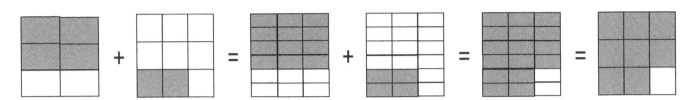

$$\frac{4}{6} + \frac{2}{9} = \frac{12}{18} + \frac{4}{18} = \frac{16}{18} = \frac{8}{9}$$

$$0.\dot{6} + 0.\dot{2} = 0.\dot{6} + 0.\dot{2} = 0.\dot{8} = 0.\dot{8}$$

$$\frac{}{} + \frac{}{} = \frac{}{} + \frac{}{} = \frac{}{}$$

$$\underline{\quad\quad} + \underline{\quad\quad} = \underline{\quad\quad} + \underline{\quad\quad} = \underline{\quad\quad}$$

Complete the following visual fraction additions.
Fill in blank spaces with missing fractions and decimal fractions, as applicable

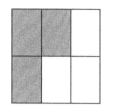 + 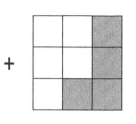 = 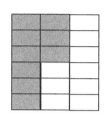 + 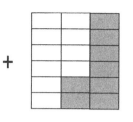 =

$$\frac{3}{6} + \frac{4}{9} = \frac{9}{18} + \frac{8}{18} = \frac{17}{18}$$

$$0.50 \quad + \quad 0.4\dot{} \quad = \quad 0.50 \quad + \quad 0.4\dot{} \quad = \quad 0.94\dot{}$$

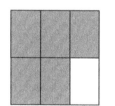 + 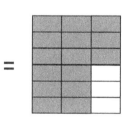 = 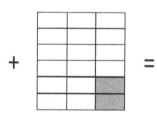 +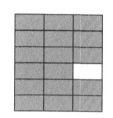

$$\text{—} \quad + \quad \text{—} \quad = \quad \text{—} \quad + \quad \text{—} \quad = \quad \text{—}$$

$$\text{--} \blacksquare \text{-----}\dot{} \quad + \quad \text{--}\blacksquare\text{-----}\dot{} \quad = \quad \text{--}\blacksquare\text{-----}\dot{} \quad + \quad \text{--}\blacksquare\text{-----}\dot{} \quad = \quad \text{--}\blacksquare\text{-----}\dot{}$$

Complete the following visual fraction additions.

Fill in blanks with missing fractions and decimal fractions, as applicable

$$\frac{2}{6} + \frac{6}{9} = \frac{6}{18} + \frac{12}{18} = \frac{18}{18} = 1$$

$$0.3\dot{} + 0.6\dot{} = 0.3\dot{} + 0.6\dot{} = 1.00 = 1.00$$

$$\frac{}{} + \frac{}{} = \frac{}{} + \frac{}{} = \frac{}{} = \text{-----}$$

$$\text{--.----} \dot{} + \text{--.----} \dot{} = \text{--.----} \dot{} + \text{--.----} \dot{} = \text{--.-----} = \text{--.-----}$$

Thirds + Sixths + Ninths

Complete the following visual fraction additions.
Fill in blank spaces with missing fractions and decimal fractions, as applicable

$$\frac{0}{3} + \frac{0}{6} + \frac{0}{9} = \frac{0}{18} + \frac{0}{18} + \frac{0}{18} = \frac{0}{18} = 0$$

$$0.00 + 0.00 + 0.00 = 0.00 + 0.00 + 0.00 = 0.00 = 0$$

$$— + — + — = — + — + — = —$$

$$\_.\_\_\_ + \_.\_\_\_ + \_.\_\_\_ = \_.\_\_\_ + \_.\_\_\_ + \_.\_\_\_ = \_.\_\_\_$$

Complete the following visual fraction additions.
Fill in blanks with missing fractions and decimal fractions, as applicable

$$\frac{1}{3} + \frac{1}{6} + \frac{2}{9} = \frac{6}{18} + \frac{3}{18} + \frac{4}{18} = \frac{13}{18}$$

$$0.3\dot{} + 0.16\dot{} + 0.2\dot{} = 0.3\dot{} + 0.16\dot{} + 0.2\dot{} = 0.72\dot{}$$

$$\frac{\quad}{\quad} + \frac{\quad}{\quad} + \frac{\quad}{\quad} = \frac{\quad}{\quad} + \frac{\quad}{\quad} + \frac{\quad}{\quad} = \frac{\quad}{\quad} = \frac{\quad}{\quad}$$

$$\underline{\quad}\dot{} + \underline{\quad}\dot{} + \underline{\quad}\dot{} = \underline{\quad}\dot{} + \underline{\quad}\dot{} + \underline{\quad}\dot{} = \underline{\quad}\dot{} = \underline{\quad}\dot{}$$

83

Complete the following visual fraction additions.
Fill in blank spaces with missing fractions and decimal fractions, as applicable

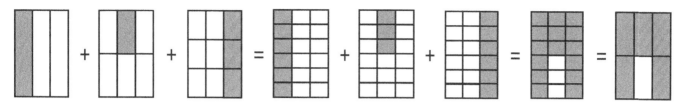

$$\frac{1}{3} + \frac{1}{6} + \frac{3}{9} = \frac{6}{18} + \frac{3}{18} + \frac{6}{18} = \frac{15}{18} = \frac{5}{6}$$

$$0.3\dot{} + 0.16\dot{} + 0.3\dot{} = 0.3\dot{} + 0.16\dot{} + 0.3\dot{} = 0.83\dot{} = 0.83\dot{}$$

$$— + — + — = — + — + — = — = —$$

$$\_\_.\_\_\dot{} + \_\_.\_\_\dot{} + \_\_.\_\_\dot{} = \_\_.\_\_\dot{} + \_\_.\_\_\dot{} + \_\_.\_\_\dot{} = \_\_.\_\_\dot{} = \_\_.\_\_\dot{}$$

Complete the following visual fraction additions.
Fill in blanks with missing fractions and decimal fractions, as applicable

$$\frac{1}{3} + \frac{1}{6} + \frac{4}{9} = \frac{6}{18} + \frac{3}{18} + \frac{8}{18} = \frac{17}{18}$$

$$0.3\dot{} + 0.16\dot{} + 0.4\dot{} = 0.3\dot{} + 0.16\dot{} + 0.4\dot{} = 0.94\dot{}$$

$$\frac{}{} + \frac{}{} + \frac{}{} = \frac{}{} + \frac{}{} + \frac{}{} = \frac{}{}$$

$$\_\_\blacksquare\_\_\dot{} + \_\_\blacksquare\_\_\dot{} + \_\_\blacksquare\_\_\dot{} = \_\_\blacksquare\_\_\dot{} + \_\_\blacksquare\_\_\dot{} + \_\_\blacksquare\_\_\dot{} = \_\_\blacksquare\_\_\dot{}$$

Complete the following visual fraction additions.
Fill in blank spaces with missing fractions and decimal fractions, as applicable

$$\frac{2}{3} + \frac{1}{6} + \frac{1}{9} = \frac{12}{18} + \frac{3}{18} + \frac{2}{18} = \frac{17}{18}$$

$$0.6^{.} + 0.16^{.} + 0.1^{.} = 0.6^{.} + 0.16^{.} + 0.1^{.} = 0.94^{.}$$

$$\frac{}{} + \frac{}{} + \frac{}{} = \frac{}{} + \frac{}{} + \frac{}{} = \frac{}{} = \text{\_\_\_\_}$$

$$\_.\_\_\_^{.} + \_.\_\_\_^{.} + \_.\_\_\_^{.} = \_.\_\_\_^{.} + \_.\_\_\_^{.} + \_.\_\_\_^{.} = \_\_.\_\_\_\_ = \_\_.\_\_\_\_$$

Quiz 2

Match each fraction **sum** with its **answers**.

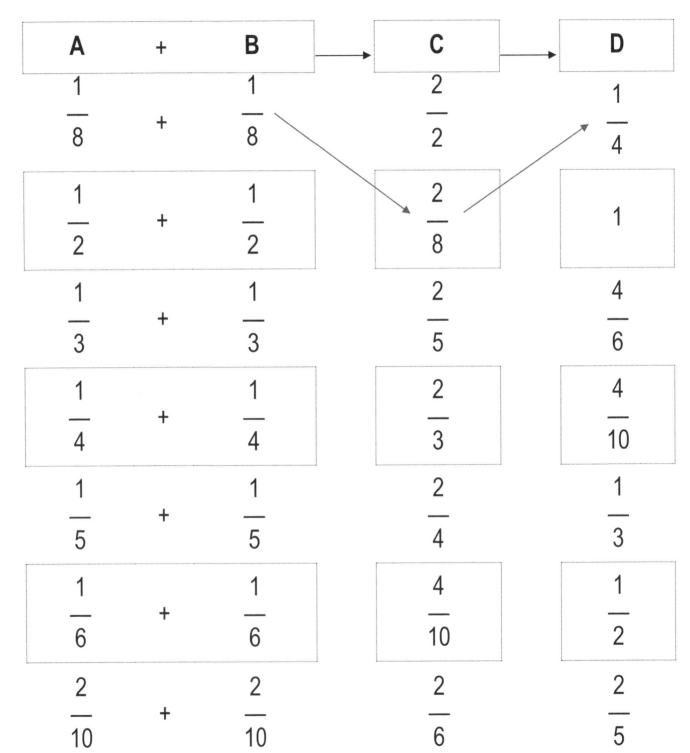

A	+	B	→	C	→	D
$\frac{1}{8}$	+	$\frac{1}{8}$		$\frac{2}{2}$		$\frac{1}{4}$
$\frac{1}{2}$	+	$\frac{1}{2}$		$\frac{2}{8}$		1
$\frac{1}{3}$	+	$\frac{1}{3}$		$\frac{2}{5}$		$\frac{4}{6}$
$\frac{1}{4}$	+	$\frac{1}{4}$		$\frac{2}{3}$		$\frac{4}{10}$
$\frac{1}{5}$	+	$\frac{1}{5}$		$\frac{2}{4}$		$\frac{1}{3}$
$\frac{1}{6}$	+	$\frac{1}{6}$		$\frac{4}{10}$		$\frac{1}{2}$
$\frac{2}{10}$	+	$\frac{2}{10}$		$\frac{2}{6}$		$\frac{2}{5}$

Adding **Like Fractions**

Fractions with **like denominators** (same bottom numbers) can be easily added (or subtracted).

Example, $\dfrac{1}{4} + \dfrac{1}{4}$ or

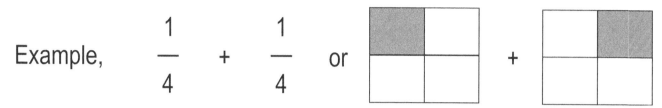

i) Add numerators (top numbers) together.

$$\frac{1}{\_} + \frac{1}{\_} = \frac{2}{\_} \rightarrow$$

ii) Use the **common** denominator (bottom number shared by fractions).

So, $\dfrac{1}{\_} + \dfrac{1}{\_} = \dfrac{2}{\_}$ becomes $\dfrac{2 \leftarrow \textbf{numerators} \text{ added}}{4 \leftarrow \text{common } \textbf{denominator}}$

i.e.   ☐ + ☐ = ☐   changes to ☐

The **denominator** stays the **same** – not added like the numerators.

iii) If possible, simplify the result by dividing both the numerator and the denominator by the same **factor** (number).

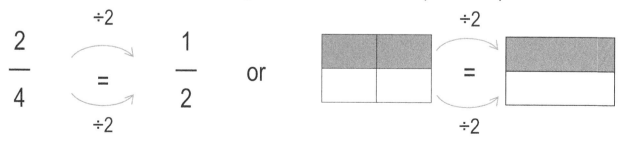

$\dfrac{2}{4} = \dfrac{1}{2}$ or

Simplifying Fractions

Compare the numerators and the denominators to simplify.

$$\frac{1}{2} + \frac{1}{2} = \frac{2}{2} = 1 \rightarrow$$

Think about division as grouping, and use this to simplify fractions.

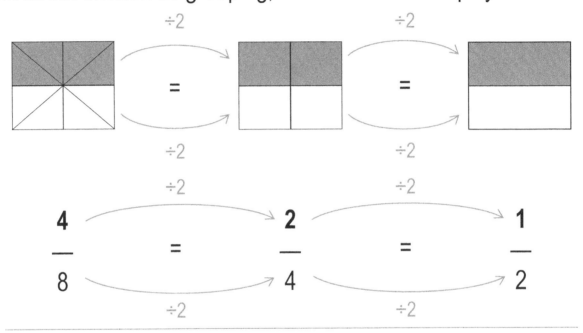

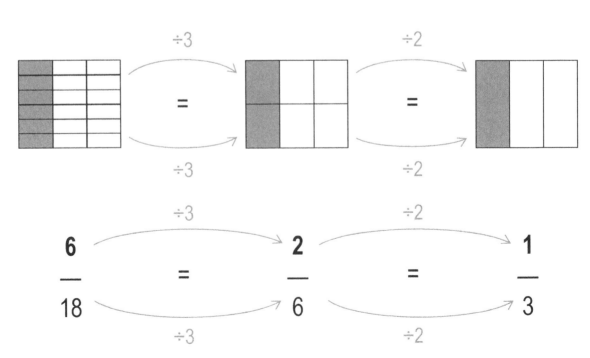

Adding **Unlike Fractions** Tutorial

Fractions with **unlike denominators** (different bottom numbers) need to be adjusted to have the **same** denominators to add them together.

Stage 1
Make the **denominators** (bottom numbers) the same.
This is called finding the **common denominator**.

To do this, you need to find the **lowest common multiple** (LCM) of the bottom numbers of the fractions to be added. LCM is the *smallest* whole number which both of the denominators will divide exactly into.

$$\frac{1}{2} \quad + \quad \frac{2}{4} \quad =$$

4 can be divided by 2 and by 4 itself. So in the above example, **4** is the LCM and could be used as the **common** denominator.

LCM can be found using **times tables** or **multiplication** lists.

Stage 2
Use the LCM to adjust both the **denominator** and the **numerator**.
You have to multiply both the top and the bottom of the fraction by the same number to keep the fraction value the same; *equivalent fraction*.

$$\frac{1}{2} \quad \begin{array}{c} \times 2 \\ = \\ \times 2 \end{array} \quad \frac{2}{4} \qquad \text{or}$$

Stage 3
Add the **numerators** together and use the **common** denominator.

So, $\dfrac{2}{4} + \dfrac{2}{4}$ becomes $\dfrac{4}{4}$ ← **Numerators** addend

← Common **denominator**

equals

Stage 4
If possible, simplify the result *(divide top and bottom the same factor)*.

$\dfrac{4}{4}$ $\xrightarrow{\div 2}$ $=$ $\xrightarrow{\div 2}$ $\dfrac{2}{2}$ $\xrightarrow{\div 2}$ $=$ $\xrightarrow{\div 2}$ 1

$=$ $=$

Putting it all together

$$\frac{1}{2} + \frac{2}{4} = \frac{2}{4} + \frac{2}{4} = \frac{2+2}{4} = \frac{4}{4} = 1$$

Examples

Some examples of adding fractions with *different* denominators.

Example A

Solve: $\dfrac{1}{2} + \dfrac{2}{4}$

Find the LCM of **2** and **4**.

2 times table	=	0	2	**4**	6	8 ...
4 times table	=	0		**4**		8 ...

4 is the first number that appears in both the 2 and the 4 times table or multiplication list. That means, it is the **lowest common multiple**. So, the lowest common multiple (LCM) of 2 and 4 is **4**.

$$\frac{1}{2} + \frac{2}{4} \rightarrow \frac{2}{4} + \frac{2}{4} = \frac{4}{4} = 1$$

Example B

Solve: $\dfrac{1}{4} + \dfrac{5}{8}$

Find the LCM of **4** and **8**.

4 times table	=	0	4	**8**	12	16 ...
8 times table	=	0		**8**		16 ...

92

8 is the lowest multiple in both the 4 times table and the 8 times table. Therefore, **8** is the LCM of 4 and 8.

$$\frac{1}{4} + \frac{5}{8} \rightarrow \frac{2}{8} + \frac{5}{8} = \frac{7}{8}$$

Example C

Solve:	$\frac{1}{2}$	+	$\frac{1}{4}$	+	$\frac{1}{8}$

Find the LCM of **2**, **4** and **8**.

2 times table	=	0	2	4	6	**8**	...
4 times table	=	0		4		**8**	...
8 times table	=	0				**8**	...

8 is the first number to appear in *all* 2, 4 and 8 times tables.
So, it is the lowest common multiple (LCM) of 2, 4 and 8.

$$\frac{1}{2} + \frac{1}{4} + \frac{1}{8} \rightarrow \frac{4}{8} + \frac{2}{8} + \frac{1}{8} = \frac{7}{8}$$

Example D

Solve:	$\frac{2}{5}$	+	$\frac{5}{10}$

Find the LCM of **5** and **10**.

5 times table	=	0	5	**10**	...
10 times table	=	0		**10**	...

The first multiple to appear in both the 5 and the 10 times tables is **10**. So, **10** is the lowest common multiple (LCM) of 5 and 10.

$$\frac{2}{5} + \frac{5}{10} \rightarrow \frac{4}{10} + \frac{5}{10} = \frac{9}{10}$$

Example E

Solve: $\dfrac{1}{3} + \dfrac{2}{6}$

Find the LCM of **3** and **6**.

3 times table	=	0		3		**6**	…
6 times table	=	0				**6**	…

6 appears in both 3 and 6 times tables or multiplication lists. Consequently, the LCM of 3 and 6 is **6**.

$$\frac{1}{3} + \frac{2}{6} \rightarrow \frac{2}{6} + \frac{2}{6} = \frac{4}{6} = \frac{2}{3}$$

Example F

Solve: $\dfrac{1}{6} + \dfrac{2}{9}$

Find the LCM of **6** and **9**.

6 times table	=	0		6		12		**18**	…
9 times table	=	0				9		**18**	…

The multiples of 6 and 9 first match at **18**.
So, the LCM of 6 and 9 is **18**.

$$\frac{1}{6} + \frac{2}{9} \rightarrow \frac{3}{18} + \frac{4}{18} = \frac{7}{18}$$

Example G

Solve: $\quad \dfrac{1}{3} \quad + \quad \dfrac{1}{6} \quad + \quad \dfrac{1}{9}$

Find the LCM of **3**, **6** and **9**.

3 times table	= 0	3	6	9	12	15	**18** ...

6 times table	= 0		6		12		**18** ...

9 times table	= 0			9			**18** ...

18 is the first multiple to appear in *all* three times tables.
Therefore, the LCM of 3, 6 and 9 is **18**.

$$\frac{1}{3} + \frac{1}{6} + \frac{1}{9} \rightarrow \frac{6}{18} + \frac{3}{18} + \frac{2}{18} = \frac{11}{18}$$

More examples

Here are some other examples of adding *unlike* fractions with *different* denominators.

$$\frac{2}{4} + \frac{2}{8} = \frac{4}{8} + \frac{2}{8} = \frac{4+2}{8} = \frac{6}{8} = \frac{3}{4}$$

$$\frac{1}{2} + \frac{1}{4} + \frac{1}{8} = \frac{4}{8} + \frac{2}{8} + \frac{1}{8} = \frac{4+2+1}{6} = \frac{7}{8}$$

$$\frac{1}{5} + \frac{3}{10} = \frac{2}{10} + \frac{3}{10} = \frac{2+3}{10} = \frac{5}{10} = \frac{1}{2}$$

$$\frac{1}{3} + \frac{2}{6} = \frac{2}{6} + \frac{2}{6} = \frac{2+2}{6} = \frac{4}{6} = \frac{2}{3}$$

$$\frac{3}{6} + \frac{3}{9} = \frac{9}{18} + \frac{6}{18} = \frac{9+6}{18} = \frac{15}{18} = \frac{5}{6}$$

$$\frac{1}{3} + \frac{1}{6} + \frac{1}{9} = \frac{6}{18} + \frac{3}{18} + \frac{2}{18} = \frac{6+3+2}{18} = \frac{11}{18}$$

SUMMARY

When all the denominators are in the same times table (list of multiples), the bigger or biggest one in the list is their LCM.

Example

×**2** table	=	0	2	4	6	**8** ...
×**4** table	=	0		4		**8** ...
×**8** table	=	0				**8** ...

LCM of 2 and 4 is **4**.
LCM of 4 and 8 is **8**.
LCM of 2, 4 and 8 is **8**.

×**5** table	=	0	5	**10** ...
×**10** table	=	0		**10** ...

LCM of 5 and 10 is **10**.

If, however, all the denominators are *not* in the same times table, then their LCM is the **first** number at which all their times tables **match**.

×**3** table	=	0	3	**6**	9	12	15	**18** ...
×**6** table	=	0		**6**		12		**18** ...
×**9** table	=	0			9			**18** ...

The LCM of 3 & 6 is **6**. LCM of 6 & 9 is **18**. And LCM of 3, 6 & 9 is **18**.

After you have made the denominators the same, the rest of the adding process is the same as for *Adding Like Fractions* (see section above) on page 89.

So, you first convert the *unlike* fractions you are adding into equivalent fractions. You then add (or subtract) *like* fractions. That's it.

Create Your Own Visual Maths Fractions
Invent your very own fractions to **complete**, then **colour** and/or **shade**
Make them more fun, interesting and different. Go on, get creative!

HALVES

 + 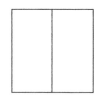 = =

$\dfrac{\quad}{2}$ + $\dfrac{\quad}{2}$ = $\dfrac{\quad}{2}$ = $\dfrac{\quad}{\quad}$

0.___ + 0.___ = 0.___ = ___

QUARTERS

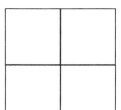 + 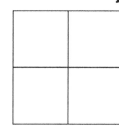 = 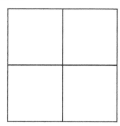 =

$\dfrac{\quad}{4}$ + $\dfrac{\quad}{4}$ = $\dfrac{\quad}{4}$ = $\dfrac{\quad}{\quad}$

0.___ + 0.___ = 0.___ = ___

EIGHTHS

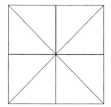 + 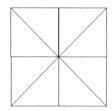 = 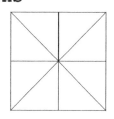 =

$\dfrac{\quad}{8}$ + $\dfrac{\quad}{8}$ = $\dfrac{\quad}{8}$ = $\dfrac{\quad}{\quad}$

0.___ + 0.___ = 0.___ = ___

HALVES + QUARTERS

$$\frac{}{2} + \frac{}{4} = \frac{}{4} + \frac{}{4} = \frac{}{} = \frac{}{}$$

0.___ + 0.___ = 0.___ + 0.___ = 0.___ = ___

HALVES + EIGHTHS

$$\frac{}{2} + \frac{}{8} = \frac{}{8} + \frac{}{8} = \frac{}{} = \frac{}{}$$

0.___ + 0.___ = 0.___ + 0.___ = 0.___ = ___

HALVES + QUARTERS + EIGHTHS

$$\frac{}{2} + \frac{}{4} + \frac{}{8} = \frac{}{8} + \frac{}{8} + \frac{}{8} = \frac{}{}$$

0.___ + 0.___ + 0.___ = 0.___ + 0.___ + 0.___ = ___

FIFTHS

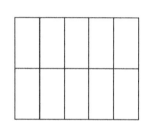 + 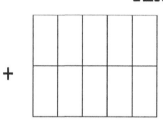 = 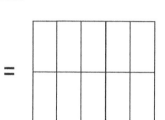 =

$$\frac{\quad}{5} \quad + \quad \frac{\quad}{5} \quad = \quad \frac{\quad}{5} \quad = \quad \underline{\quad}$$

$$0.\underline{\quad} \quad + \quad 0.\underline{\quad} \quad = \quad 0.\underline{\quad} \quad = \quad \underline{\quad}$$

TENTHS

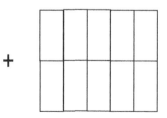 + 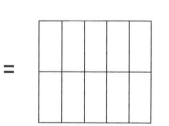 = 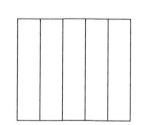 =

$$\frac{\quad}{10} \quad + \quad \frac{\quad}{10} \quad = \quad \frac{\quad}{10} \quad = \quad \underline{\quad}$$

$$0.\underline{\quad} \quad + \quad 0.\underline{\quad} \quad = \quad 0.\underline{\quad} \quad = \quad \underline{\quad}$$

$$\frac{\quad}{10} \quad + \quad \frac{\quad}{10} \quad = \quad \frac{\quad}{10} \quad = \quad \frac{\quad}{5}$$

$$0.\underline{\quad} \quad + \quad 0.\underline{\quad} \quad = \quad 0.\underline{\quad} \quad = \quad 0.\underline{\quad}$$

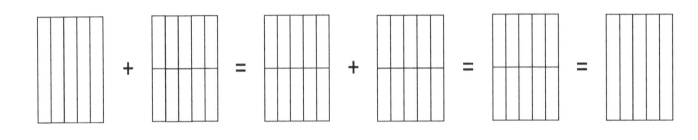

$$\frac{}{5} \quad + \quad \frac{}{10} \quad = \quad \frac{}{10} \quad + \quad \frac{}{10} \quad = \quad \frac{}{10} \quad = \quad \underline{}$$

$$0.\underline{} \quad + \quad 0.\underline{} \quad = \quad 0.\underline{} \quad + \quad 0.\underline{} \quad = \quad 0.\underline{} \quad = \quad \underline{}$$

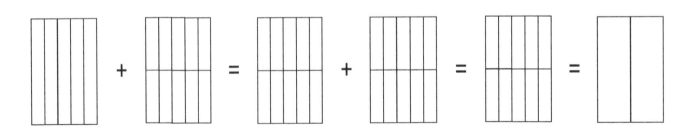

$$\frac{}{5} \quad + \quad \frac{}{10} \quad = \quad \frac{}{10} \quad + \quad \frac{}{10} \quad = \quad \frac{}{10} \quad = \quad \frac{}{5}$$

$$0.\underline{} \quad + \quad 0.\underline{} \quad = \quad 0.\underline{} \quad + \quad 0.\underline{} \quad = \quad 0.\underline{} \quad = \quad \underline{}$$

$$\frac{}{5} \quad + \quad \frac{}{10} \quad = \quad \frac{}{10} \quad + \quad \frac{}{10} \quad = \quad \frac{}{10} \quad = \quad \frac{1}{2}$$

$$0.\underline{} \quad + \quad 0.\underline{} \quad = \quad 0.\underline{} \quad + \quad 0.\underline{} \quad = \quad 0.\underline{} \quad = \quad 0.\underline{}$$

THIRDS

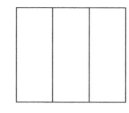

$$\frac{\ \ }{3} \quad + \quad \frac{\ \ }{3} \quad = \quad \frac{\ \ }{3} \quad = \quad \frac{\ \ }{\ \ }$$

$$0.\underline{\ \ \ } \quad + \quad 0.\underline{\ \ \ } \quad = \quad 0.\underline{\ \ \ } \quad = \quad \underline{\ \ \ }$$

SIXTHS

 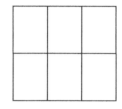 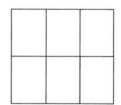 

$$\frac{\ \ }{6} \quad + \quad \frac{\ \ }{6} \quad = \quad \frac{\ \ }{6} \quad = \quad \frac{\ \ }{\ \ }$$

$$0.\underline{\ \ \ } \quad + \quad 0.\underline{\ \ \ } \quad = \quad 0.\underline{\ \ \ } \quad = \quad \underline{\ \ \ }$$

NINTHS

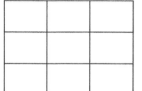 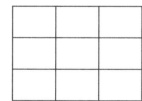 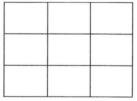

$$\frac{\ \ }{9} \quad + \quad \frac{\ \ }{9} \quad = \quad \frac{\ \ }{9} \quad = \quad \frac{\ \ }{\ \ }$$

$$0.\underline{\ \ \ } \quad + \quad 0.\underline{\ \ \ } \quad = \quad 0.\underline{\ \ \ } \quad = \quad \underline{\ \ \ }$$

THIRDS + SIXTHS

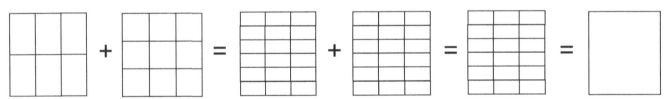

$$\frac{\;}{3} + \frac{\;}{6} = \frac{\;}{6} + \frac{\;}{6} = \frac{\;}{6} = \frac{\;}{\;}$$

THIRDS + NINTHS

$$\frac{\;}{3} + \frac{\;}{9} = \frac{\;}{9} + \frac{\;}{9} = \frac{\;}{9} = \frac{\;}{\;}$$

SIXTHS + NINTHS

$$\frac{\;}{6} + \frac{\;}{9} = \frac{\;}{18} + \frac{\;}{18} = \frac{\;}{18} = \frac{\;}{\;}$$

THIRDS + SIXTHS + NINTHS

$$\frac{\;}{3} + \frac{\;}{6} + \frac{\;}{9} = \frac{\;}{18} + \frac{\;}{18} + \frac{\;}{18} = \frac{\;}{18} = \frac{\;}{\;}$$

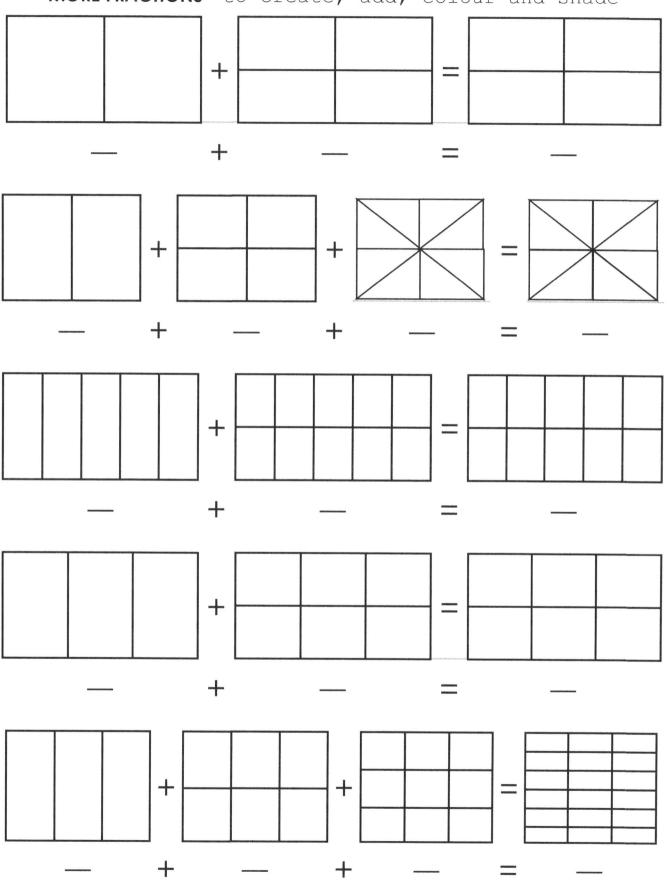

author.to/FractionsVisually | https://fractionsvisually.com

Thank you for buying my book and helping the author to keep on writing. ☺
I hope you've enjoyed reading **ADDING** FRACTIONS VISUALLY WORKBOOK.
If so, please, kindly consider leaving a review on **Amazon.com** at
amazon.com/review/create-review?&asin=1729562493.

A single line, short sentence, few phrases or just rating will do.
No need overthink of what to write, how much or how little.

If not, please, send me your feedback, comments and corrections to:
eng-s-jama@fractionsvisually.com.
Thanks.

Series 1: **UNDERSTANDING** FRACTIONS VISUALLY
    Colouring workbook: mybook.to/WB1-Sh-v2
    Paperback: mybook.to/B-1
    Colour paperback: mybook.to/B1-C
    Colour ebook: mybook.to/eB1-C
    Workbook: mybook.to/WB-1
    Colour workbook: mybook.to/WB1-C

Series 2: **ADDING** FRACTIONS VISUALLY
    Colouring workbook: mybook.to/WB2-Sh
    Paperback: mybook.to/B-2
    Colour paperback: mybook.to/B2-C
    Colour ebook: mybook.to/eB2-C
    Workbook: mybook.to/WB2
    Colour workbook: mybook.to/WB2-C

Series 3: **ADDING FRACTIONS** *STEP-**BY**-STEP*
    Paperback: mybook.to/B-3
    Colour paperback: mybook.to/B3-C
    Workbook: mybook.to/WB3
    Colour workbook: mybook.to/WB3-C

Series 4: **UNDERSTAND, ADD & SUBTRACT** FRACTIONS VISUALLY
    Paperback: mybook.to/B-4
    Colour paperback: mybook.to/B4-C

ADDING FRACTIONS VISUALLY
Third Edition
WORKBOOK

Ages 5-11, **Grades** K-5th grade and **Years** 1-6

Complete <u>blank spaces</u> with missing **fractions**, **equivalent** fractions, **decimal** fractions and **percentages**

Create your very own **fractions** to **complete**, **colour** & **shade**
(Blank shapes and equations templates provided) ☺

Friendly **introductions** to **adding** fractions

Easy language; **illustrated** throughout

Explores and demonstrates visual **equivalent** fractions

Compares fractions, decimals and **percentages**

Uses distinct **shapes** to distinguish different denominations

Shows proper fraction, **name** and decimal equivalent of every fraction – *from nothing to whole!*

Quick quiz es to check learners' understanding & progress

Visual fractions, sums and simple maths vocabulary

Step-by-step **tutorials** on adding like fractions and adding unlike fractions

Guides students through finding the **Lowest Common Multiple** (LCM)

Amazon Marketplaces:

author.to/FractionsVisually

mybook.to/WB2

amazon.co.uk/FractionsVisually

Eng S Jama

Made in the USA
Monee, IL
09 August 2023

40729494R00059